THE
CONNECTOR
EFFECT™

THE CONNECTOR EFFECT™

The Proven Way to Grow Your Business Right Now

Ivan Misner, Ph.D.
Graham Weihmiller, MBA, CFE
with **Robert Skrob**

The Connector Effect™
The Proven Way to Grow Your Business Right Now
™ and © by BNI Global, LLC and Ivan Misner, Ph.D.
All Rights Reserved

Published by BNI Global, LLC

ISBN-13: 978-1-7355629-0-2

LCCN: 2020916310

This publication is designed to provide accurate and authoritative information in regard to the subject matter covered. It is sold with the understanding that the publisher is not engaged in rendering legal, accounting or other professional services. If legal advice or other expert assistance is required, the services of a competent professional should be sought.

To all BNI Leaders, past and present, we stand on your shoulders and we salute your terrific contributions to our collective cause.

We care about you. We hope this book helps you grow your business and make your dreams come true.

Special Recognition

The authors thank the following individuals who contributed ideas, experience and insight that made this book as great as it is.

BNI Editorial Team:
Claire Sherman and Terry Atkins

BNI Content Team:
Andy Hart, Bharat Daga, Charlie Lawson, Dan Haggerty, Meaghan Chitwood, Robert Gorecki, Tim Roberts and Vince Vigneri

And to the hundreds of BNI Members who submitted their story for consideration. For each story included in this book, there are hundreds more submitted by BNI Members around the world. Your contributions improved this book.

Table of Contents

Chapter 1

The Most Effective Way to Get New Customers[1]

"Have a seat over there. I'll let Ms. Overton know you are here," the office manager says.

You are in the waiting room with only the office manager. He busies himself on his computer. Hopefully letting Melissa Overton know you are here and waiting. You hope this meeting is different than your other meetings lately; a series of "no thank you's" and "let me think about it's."

This meeting is a huge opportunity for you. You told your spouse about it last night, and you know you'll have questions to answer about how it went when you return home this evening.

The office manager looks up and lets you know Ms. Overton is ready to see you.

It's show time. You've prepared for this opportunity. It's the first time you've met her. You have your presentation on how you can help her company save a lot of money, and you know just what to say.

But one problem has been nagging at you for the two days since you set this appointment: How do you get her to choose you?

---

[1] It may be common in your business to refer to your customers as clients, patients, guests, buyers, diners, investors, shoppers, patrons or any number of names. For the purposes of this book, we'll use one term, customer. Please translate customer into the term that best fits the name you use.

Too many of your competitors make bigger promises than you do. Others give a lowball price for which they know they can't deliver. And still others out-promise and out-price them. The fact that they don't deliver is beside the point; the deal is theirs.

This time must be different. This is a make or break moment: It's time to close this deal or go get a job somewhere else. Owning your own business has been great. But maybe it's not for you. It has been tough going up until now. You see others winning; maybe now it's your turn.

Now you have an advantage you've never had before.

You enter Ms. Overton's office and see she's still on the phone. Evidently she's multitasking at your expense because she's not ending her call.

She waves you in and points to a chair, inviting you to take a seat at a table in the corner of her office while she finishes her call.

Awkwardly, you try to not pay attention to her call. Instead, you try to distract yourself by looking at the empty walls in her office. She's new here. She hasn't even had time to decorate.

You overhear Ms. Overton say to someone on the phone: "I'm new here. I just started a new job. How am I supposed to get work done and clean out Mom and Dad's home?"

You realize she's talking to a sibling. They lost their mom recently. Melissa moved to town. She took a new job. This was all so she could help take care of her dad.

But his condition has deteriorated. It's more than she can handle.

"He's fine right now; there's no way he can go back home now that Mom is gone," she says.

Suddenly self-conscious in your presence, she says, "I can't talk anymore right now. Let's discuss it tonight and figure out what to do."

She taps her phone to end the call, sets it on her desk and walks over to you with her hand extended, saying, "Hello, my name is Melissa Overton. It's a pleasure to meet you. Sorry I was running late. How can I help you?"

"Melissa, I couldn't help but overhear you are going through a difficult time with your family right now. It's not what I came here to discuss, but because I belong to a BNI® Chapter here in town I have an extensive network of people you can trust to help you relocate your father. Would you like me to pull out my phone and get you connected with them?"

"Oh my gosh, yes! You are a life saver," she responds.

Over the next 20 minutes, you open up the BNI Connect® app on your phone. You refer her to a long-term care consultant to help her find a great home for her father, a real estate professional to list his current home for sale, a moving company to pack up his belongings and an attorney to take care of the necessary legal paperwork.

Serendipitously, you just learned what an adult child with an aging parent needs when you attended your BNI Chapter meeting earlier this week. George Johnson, a member of your BNI Chapter, gave a short presentation on the challenges of dealing with aging parents as part of the meeting. Although you aren't in that situation yourself right now, you have the information to help Melissa. That presentation is the reason you knew the steps to take and the people to call.

But shoot. Between the meeting starting late because of her phone call and your efforts to give her the referrals she needed, your time is up.

Melissa says, "Thank you for all this. Can you tell me in two minutes why you came here today?"

Two minutes doesn't do it justice. But you give it your best shot. And as she walks you out so she can take her next appointment, Melissa thanks you and tells you she'll be in touch.

While you get a rewarding feeling from passing referrals to close friends in your BNI Chapter, you didn't get the deal you came for. And you'll have to figure out how to explain it all when you get home tonight.

Later that afternoon the office manager calls you back. He wants you to email over your agreement. He tells you, "Each of the people you referred to Ms. Overton couldn't stop talking about how great you are at what you do. She asked me to hire you right away."

You did it! Melissa is ready to sign with you, and she needs you to send the paperwork.

Your BNI referral network gave you the trusted contacts you needed to solve Melissa's problem. Your BNI Chapter members extolled you for what you did for them. That fostered more trust than any sales presentation could have. Because you were a member of your BNI Chapter, you got the business over everyone else.

And it happened by you giving first—by giving without expectation of anything in return. You put the Givers Gain® principle into action.
Those who give first get the most.

Those who give first get the most.

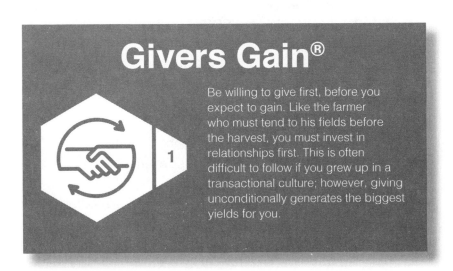

Givers Gain®

Be willing to give first, before you expect to gain. Like the farmer who must tend to his fields before the harvest, you must invest in relationships first. This is often difficult to follow if you grew up in a transactional culture; however, giving unconditionally generates the biggest yields for you.

How to be a Master Connector™:
Be the Person Who Gets the Business Because of Who You Know

Your BNI Chapter gives you a network you can trust to refer your friends, family and best customers. This is a group of businesspeople you trust to do what they promise. And because they trust you to do the same, they pass referrals from their friends, family and customers to you.

This book reveals a way of doing business that's completely different from anything you may have experienced. It's about growing your business by fostering close, personal relationships with your customers. It's about creating those relationships by being the person everyone calls when they need a problem solved. And with your network of trustworthy businesspeople within your BNI Chapter, you always know exactly who to call to get that problem solved.

It doesn't matter whether the problem is related to legal issues, financial planning, construction jobs, plumbing or automobile repair, you will always know who to call. That puts you in a powerful position within your community; you are someone others seek out for advice and contacts.

While other people seek recommendations by posting on social media, you have someone who is standing by to take your call. They are ready to help you, your friends and your customers with whatever they need. And they deliver on their promises so you always look great by giving the referral.

This book reveals exactly how you can become a Master Connector™. This is the person who builds trust by giving referrals. As a Master Connector, you can solve any problem by tapping into your vast network of businesspeople. And this grows your business effortlessly because you have earned the trust of your network.

As a Master Connector, you can solve any problem
by tapping into your vast network of businesspeople.
And this grows your business effortlessly because
you have earned the trust of your network.

And your network is trained and motivated to pass you
qualified referrals who are a perfect fit for your business
because they want to put the Givers Gain formula into
action for themselves. When an entire network practices
Givers Gain, businesses can grow faster (and larger) than
you ever thought possible.

**A Single Mom of Three Who Was Just Diagnosed With
Breast Cancer Has Her Best Month Ever, Less Than
Five Months After Becoming a Master Connector**

Even though Michelle King has lived in Birmingham,
Alabama, for more than 15 years, she didn't find her
"place" until joining the BNI Regency Chapter six months
ago.

She'd grown frustrated in the mortgage industry.
She wasn't motivated anymore and was often feeling
depressed about how difficult it was to meet people. She
was trying to make cold calls to generate new business.
Her production was low, as was her self-esteem.

As a single parent to three boys, it had never been
easy for Michelle to balance her work with being a mom.
And then, BAM, she was diagnosed with breast cancer,
as if she needed more to worry about! Trying to stay
positive and confident enough to sell her home loan
services felt nearly impossible.

While working on a closing for a friend, she met a real estate professional, Mary Bell. Mary was able to save the deal even after the title company had "issues." Mary said, "I owe it all to my BNI team," so Michelle decided to check out a local BNI Chapter herself.

Michelle learned they were starting a new BNI Chapter in her area. When she found out the details, she was "all in."

Every loan officer strives to close $1 million per month in deals; however, Michelle never dared to dream that big before.

Six months after joining her BNI Chapter, Michelle closed $1.5 million in business within a single month. And while she's proud of that achievement, the most important change is that her BNI friends helped her find her passion again.

Michelle's BNI Chapter has helped her connect with customers to build new levels of trust. Now when she hears about customers having challenges, as a Master Connector she's able to call on her referral network to help them solve those problems. She's generating referrals from the members of her BNI Chapter and using those Members to foster stronger relationships with everyone she meets.

But most important, her motivation is back—and she's having fun again. Michelle reports, "ALL of us need encouragement, support, accountability and networking for our businesses, BUT the advantage of BNI is you get all of these things AND the ability to increase your business and income as you grow! Follow the steps and you will watch everything soar from the inside out!"

Life happens to all of us. Your business is your best opportunity to achieve financial independence. However, for so many businesspeople, that career path can become a nightmare instead of a dream come true.

Michelle discovered a better way. She became a Master Connector who could solve problems for friends, family and her customers. This generated trust and attracted more customers to her. Plus, members of her BNI Chapter passed referrals to her as they encountered great customers for Michelle.

This book is an introduction and an invitation for you to have a more fulfilling and productive business. Through this book you'll have the opportunity to meet more than two dozen businesspeople from around the world. They are a diverse group who work in diverse industries and are from many countries. What they share is the ways they've each endeavored to become a Master Connector within their community.

Master Connectors are the people with the contacts to solve any problem. They know who to call—and when they call, the phone gets answered. It's easier for Master Connectors to build trust with people they meet because they can make valuable connections to solve problems. Master Connectors build a reputation as the person to call whenever there's a problem.

But most important, you'll discover how easy it is to become a Master Connector yourself. And how becoming a Master Connector will help you experience power, independence and fulfillment in your business life.

Chapter 2
Growing a Small Business Is Easier as a Master Connector

James Sharp has done it all to grow his real estate career. He jumped in and did what worked, according to what other real estate professionals told him. James cold called, sat at open houses hoping buyers would stop by and took several four-hour shifts at the front desk of the real estate office just to try and meet new customers. He struck out so many times he felt like a failure. In fact, he didn't sell any homes for the first six months of his career.

It all turned around when he discovered BNI. James became a Founding Member of a new BNI Chapter in the Dallas, Texas, area in 2002. In the years since, that Chapter has grown from eight Members to more than 60 today. It is one of the largest, most productive BNI Chapters in the Dallas/Fort Worth region.

But more important for James, this BNI Chapter launched his career.

Today James is the owner of The Sharp Real Estate Group. His team generated top production within his real estate company. They beat out more than 2,000 agents around the company last year. And between 50-70% of his closed business is directly attributable to referrals from his BNI Chapter.

But that's just the half of it.

James commits to giving 10 referrals each week to Members of his Chapter. This is a great goal for someone with his extensive BNI experience. He's always looking for opportunities to recommend Members of his Chapter to his clients, friends and the people he meets.

This has propelled him to Master Connector status—meaning people who know James call him with all sorts of problems, assured he'll know exactly the right person to solve it. It's free advertising for him, and it generates referrals and customers for his business each week. And it is fun and fulfilling for him.

Perhaps most important for James are the relationships he's built with fellow BNI Members. Members of his Chapter hang out together. They recently had 18 Members from the Chapter participate in a "yoga afternoon." This kind of networking allows each Member to grow a business while also fostering strong personal relationships at the same time, all while having fun together.

Through BNI, James has discovered a way he doesn't have to carry around a wall to protect himself. Instead, he can be open and giving, knowing the people around him want to build a relationship with him and see him succeed.

Today James calls himself a "Dream Maker" because he makes the dream of home ownership a reality. He feels called into this line of work to help people who don't think owning a home is possible. He wants to help them make it a reality. James is as passionate about his mission today as he was when he began 18 years ago. The only difference is, now he has the connections to make it all work.

BNI Is the Fastest Way to Become a Master Connector

The power of BNI is your local Chapter, which connects you to an international network of hundreds of thousands of businesspeople in dozens of countries around the world.

Before he started BNI, Dr. Misner went to a lot of networking groups. He found that many were very mercenary. After visiting some of them, he can still remember feeling like he needed to go home and have a shower. Everyone was so aggressive, and the meetings made him feel sleazy. One person after another was trying to sell something to him.

Then he'd visit other, more social, groups. Those groups served drinks and hors d'oeuvres. Everyone was friendly. But there was no business being done there. It was completely social. It just didn't feel like a good use of time.

Dr. Misner saw the opportunity that could exist between these distinct types of groups. He created a third type of networking group that included business and social connections, with Givers Gain® as the glue to hold these two concepts together.

The first official meeting was held in January 1985 in Arcadia, California. That first group called themselves "The Network." By the end of the year, there were 20 chapters spread throughout southern California.

By 1991, Dr. Misner could see the organization was close to growing internationally, and so to prepare for the change, he rebranded The Network as Business Network International. Shortly thereafter, he abbreviated the name to BNI for simplicity.

Together, these businesspeople pass millions of referrals generating billions of dollars in business each year.

BNI makes it much easier to become a Master Connector because your Chapter will already have many of the problem solvers you need to help your customers, friends and family. And as members of your Chapter become more familiar with you and your business, they are in a great position to refer you to their customers, friends and family.

Several decades ago BNI launched out of the simple need that faces all businesspeople: getting more new customers.

BNI was created in 1985 by Dr. Ivan Misner when he was looking for ways to generate clients for his personal consulting business.

The heart of BNI is your local BNI Chapter.

If you haven't been invited to a BNI Chapter yet, you are welcome to visit BNI.com to find one in your area. Members are excited to meet you and will make every effort to make the experience fun and productive for you.

Each Chapter allows only one member from each business category. This gives you a competitor-free environment, and it means you'll get all the referrals from the Chapter for your category. And it focuses the growth of your network on the categories you need to become a Master Connector who can solve any problem with a phone call.

Master Connectors Enjoy a Better Business Life

Hollywood movies promote the idea of the lone individual who goes out by themselves to save the world. Too many businesspeople see this as the idea, to own their own business in order to be independent of everyone else. They want to succeed by themselves.

Although the lone hero makes for dramatic movies, it's impossible to run a business like that. Eventually the lone hero will need a customer. And they will probably also need a couple of vendors to get things done. Rather than figuring it out for yourself, why not connect with a network of businesspeople who have already solved many of the problems you face?

We hear from so many businesspeople how difficult business was before they joined BNI. They tell us that life without BNI is:

- Wasting money on marketing that doesn't work
- Being on your own, trying to figure things out solo
- Being resented by those who think businesspeople take advantage of customers and employees
- Having too few, inconsistent business referrals with a weak referral network
- Seeing your unique message get lost with so many competitors clamoring for the same business
- Being on your own to develop the skills you need as you grow your business
- Dealing with "takers" who don't appreciate what you offer
- Watching goals slip by and dreams get delayed because it's easy to slack off when no one is watching

You'll hear a lot of unique stories from the hundreds of thousands of businesspeople who are BNI Members around the world. Their stories are similar in that life with BNI includes:

- A team to generate a steady flow of new customers
- Help with avoiding dead ends so you can win, faster!
- Appreciation for the sacrifices you make and the celebration of your victories
- A network of businesspeople who know how to make meaningful referrals to you and who can offer training for you on how to leverage these referrals
- You as the only provider for your business category within your Chapter—you get all the referrals from your Chapter for that category
- Comprehensive training programs that grow with you as you scale your company
- A room of "Givers" dedicated to helping you grow
- People to hold you accountable to achieve your goals and make your dreams come true

BNI Membership makes business more rewarding, and it makes life more fun.

3 BNI Secrets That Accelerate Your Business Growth

It is possible to become a Master Connector without BNI. There are individuals who do it from time to time. But it takes them years to build a network and to build trust.

However, there are three secrets, hidden in plain sight, that make BNI so effective at making you a Master Connector. We call them BNI's Hidden Secrets because they serve as the foundation of everything we do; however, they work in the background most of the time.

BNI Master Connector Secret #1

BNI is powered by "The Connector Effect™." The Connector Effect has been documented within industries as diverse as investments, computer networks and economics. It's sometimes called the network effect or Metcalf's law. The network effect is when a good or a service becomes more valuable when each additional user joins the network.

What if there's a new messaging app and you love using it? If you only have two friends who use the same messaging app, then the app has a limited value to you. However, each additional friend who installs the app makes the app more useful for each existing user. This is the same principle that drives the growth of social media platforms, as more users give you more people with whom to connect.

The same phenomenon within your referral network is called The Connector Effect. Each new connection you make increases the value of your referral network.

Each new connection you make increases the value of your referral network. BNI grows in value as your Chapter grows and you complete your network.

As your BNI Chapter continues growing, there are more businesspeople to pass you referrals. And as you fill your network with professionals within each category, it becomes easier and easier to solve problems for your customers, friends and family by referring them to Members of your BNI Chapter. BNI grows in value as your Chapter grows and you complete your network.

Most BNI Members discover they receive more referrals in the second year than they did during their first year as a BNI Member. And many find they generate more referrals in their third year than the first two years combined. This is the power of The Connector Effect in action. Each new relationship makes all of your previous relationships more valuable. As you grow your referral network, The Connector Effect kicks in to accelerate your business growth.

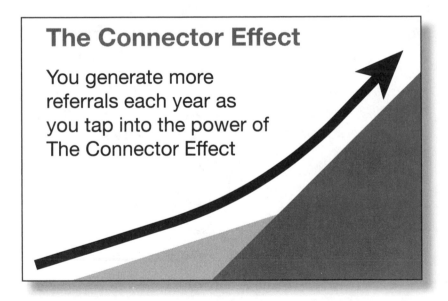

The Connector Effect

You generate more referrals each year as you tap into the power of The Connector Effect

You become a stronger Master Connector through The Connector Effect. And The Connector Effect is also the reason it's so difficult to try to become a Master Connector on your own. It's difficult to start and then grow a network by yourself—at BNI, you're not alone.

BNI Master Connector Secret #2

The next secret is that BNI makes passing referrals within your Chapter more fun in the same way that the GPS navigation software app Waze makes finding your way to your destination more fun. The more you use Waze, the higher your status. Frequent users feel good as they earn recognition and rewards. This solves an important problem most people encounter when they try to become a Master Connector without the support of a BNI Chapter.

How many times have you met a new contact who is in the perfect position to give you great referrals, but he never does? You take him to meals, and you greet him whenever you see him. But for some reason, he never gets around to passing you a referral. Or when he does, it's so weak that it has little value.

Just because someone can pass you referrals doesn't mean he will. He may not know how to pass referrals, he may be so focused on himself that he doesn't think about you or he's just not interested. Why would someone need to download and use another app for GPS directions when an app came preloaded on their phone? There's no need to use the extra storage. Waze incorporated gamification into the app so users remain loyal even though there are plenty of other options.

Waze's gamification systems encourage customers to use the app more often. There's a "scoreboard" and recognition for achieving a higher score. Plus, there's friendly competition among members to increase their own score and challenge others. When you pass another "Wazer" (the self-descriptive term for those who frequently use the app) who has more miles than you, it motivates you to use the app a little more often so you can accumulate that status, too.

Since 1985 BNI has used a scoreboard, recognition and friendly competition to increase referrals throughout their network. These practices make it fun to pass referrals to each other. It creates a team atmosphere with a room full of Givers working to grow each other's businesses. It encourages each BNI Member to learn how to pass quality referrals, to think about you when opportunities arise and to strive to pass more referrals to you.

Scores are important because you can't hit a target for which you aren't aiming. BNI Members track referrals passed as well as the dollar value of business closed as a result. This makes giving referrals fun as you compete with your Chapter Members to see who can give the most referrals.

As you give referrals, your "score" grows. And so does the friendly competition among your Chapter Members to pass you referrals for your business.

During a Chapter meeting you'll commonly hear Members talk about referral values and other statistics. This is important because everyone in the Chapter is striving to increase that score by passing more referrals.

All this creates an environment where passing quality referrals to help your fellow Members grow their business is the expectation. Your Chapter develops the skill of giving stronger referrals that convert at a higher rate than any other marketing approach.

> Your Chapter develops the skill of giving stronger referrals that convert at a higher rate than any other marketing approach.

BNI Master Connector Secret #3

The final secret is our system. You'll learn the secrets of the BNI system within the pages of this book. And it's the key reason why BNI helps you grow your business so effectively.

Over the last 35 years, in 70+ countries, there have been a lot of Chapters that have tested thousands of innovations to improve the effectiveness of the BNI system. BNI is able to measure the effectiveness of each of those variations, and each one helps BNI do more and more for BNI Members.

Through this testing process, we've discovered several proprietary processes that maximize your investment of time and accelerate your business growth as a Master Connector. You'll learn about many of these within the pages of this book.

Here are three of the most important:

Weekly Meetings – Weekly Meetings with your BNI Chapter is one of the secrets to propel you to Master Connector status. Each week you get the opportunity to describe your business and your best target customer to a room of business leaders within your community. Every detail is designed to facilitate the building of strong relationships among Members so you can grow your business by giving and receiving more referrals.

When BNI started, Weekly Meetings were based on the concept of timed-repetition. By doing things consistently and regularly, you yield greater results. This has evolved into a BNI mantra: "Do six things a thousand times, not a thousand things six times."

"Do six things a thousand times, not a thousand things six times."

Agenda – BNI Chapters use an agenda designed to grow your business. This agenda showcases you and your business. BNI Chapter meetings use an efficient agenda that compresses a lot of business growth into a short time. It makes the most of every minute you invest in your BNI Chapter.

Core Values – Throughout this book you'll see references to BNI's Core Values. These are the values that businesspeople use to accelerate everything they do in their business life and also their personal life. BNI Members use these Core Values to hold each other and themselves accountable for fostering a strong community.

You'll see them a few times within this book, but here are BNI's Core Values:

#1. Givers Gain®

Be willing to give first, before you expect to gain. Like the farmer who must tend to his fields before the harvest, you must focus on supporting other Members first. This is often difficult to follow if you grew up in a transactional culture; however, giving unconditionally generates the biggest yields for you.

#2. Building Relationships

No one is successful by themselves. Becoming good at developing relationships, creating a support network and always growing your network are the keys to success in business and in life.

#3. Lifelong Learning

Your value grows as you develop your knowledge and skills. Our world is in a constant state of change. Unless you are learning, you are falling behind. Create a curriculum based on the person you want to become and follow that curriculum to get yourself there.

#4. Traditions + Innovation

Traditions tell us who we are. Innovation tells us where we want to go. You need to know who you are as an organization, and you need to know where you are going as an organization. This keeps you from losing your place in the world while you continue to strive to create a better life for yourself and others.

#5. Positive Attitude

The habit of finding the good in everything that happens to you propels your life beyond setbacks. Those who see the best in situations, in others and in themselves magnetically attract people, opportunities and wealth.

#6. Accountability

The fastest way to build trust is to make promises and keep them. Rather than expecting others to believe and accept your word, demonstrate who you are by accepting leadership roles, following through on your promises and being the one who lives out their values, even when it appears no one is looking.

#7. Recognition

Tell the people around you that you appreciate what they've accomplished for themselves, for you and for the organization. Recognition is the fuel that builds organizations and societies. The person who masters the art of recognition attracts a strong network and leads a fulfilling life.

The Master Connector Accelerator

Within the pages of this book, you'll learn everything you need to know to become a Master Connector within your community.

These secrets will help you:

1. Make every business meeting you attend more productive in generating referrals for your business.

2. Know how to give referrals that make people eagerly want to reciprocate by passing referrals to you.

3. Create a simple template to describe your business in a way that makes it easier for others to give you referrals.

4. Know how to make yourself consistently visible so people think of you when they hear of a problem you can solve.

5. Understand the secret to growing a strong referral network so you always know exactly who to call to solve a problem.

6. Make the most of your precious time in every business situation.

7. Transform business contacts into lifelong friendships.

But first, there are a number of misconceptions about networking and business growth. Many businesspeople become trapped by these false beliefs. They try to work harder and harder, but never get ahead. Let's accelerate your success by revealing why so many other marketing approaches don't work for businesspeople today.

Chapter 3
Common Marketing Mistakes That Cause Business Failures

Too many great businesspeople could become effective Master Connectors. However, they get hung up. There's something they learned in the past or some concern they have that makes them pause. And then they miss out on a great opportunity that could make getting new customers easier for the rest of their business lives.

Here are some of the most common concerns we hear that prevent good businesspeople from becoming great Master Connectors.

"I'm going to focus on being the best in my line of business, and I'll get customers through word of mouth."

It's admirable to want to be the best at what you do. And it's important that you continue to focus on improving your craft so you are able to help the customers you seek to serve.

However, your prospective customers cannot adequately judge whether you are really better until after they buy and use the product or service. Thus, customers must rely on cues that they've learned to watch for over the years. And one of the biggest cues is "Who do you know, who is recommending you and what do they have to say about you?"

When a customer receives a recommendation from a friend that you are the best person to solve their problem, you've got a great shot at getting that person as your customer. You should continue to strive to be the best at what you do and deliver top-quality products or services. And at the same time, you should become a Master Connector so you are the person that's mentioned when someone has a problem you can solve.

"My life has completely changed," says Sandeep Chaudhry, CEO of SNP Technologies in India. Sandeep used to rely on word of mouth for his waterproofing, water treatment, swimming pool and construction products supply company. However, he didn't have a system in place. Through BNI training he learned how to ask his current clients for referrals.

Plus, he invited them as guests to his BNI Chapter. In fact, Sandeep invited more than 155 visitors to his Chapter in six years of BNI Membership. Now, more than 90-95% of his clients come from BNI, and he has a network throughout India that supports his company. The best part is his business has grown 10 times larger!

Sandeep's advice to anyone considering joining a BNI Chapter is this: "Take the plunge. Destiny has brought you to the meeting as it wants to open its gates for you."

"I'm going to become a Master Connector on my own."

While it's true you may not need BNI to pass referrals, most people discover they generate more referrals for their own business through the structure that their BNI Chapter provides. For most people who intend to do this on their own, it becomes something they don't get around to. They continue to struggle to get new customers instead of solving that problem forever by becoming a Master Connector.

When you are on your own, The Connector Effect works against you.

There are two other problems that crop up when you try to become a Master Connector on your own. When you are on your own, The Connector Effect™ works against you. With a small network, it's a challenge to establish yourself as a problem solver. You get limited referrals with only the natural referral circles of your profession.

BNI Chapters bridge across all business categories to include companies as diverse as plumbing to photography, florists and banking. Multiple categories give you a larger presence within your community. In fact, there are more than 500 categories of business professionals in BNI. This level of network diversity ensures you have the powerful referral network you need to build trust and to help someone because you always know who to call. The diverse referral network within your BNI Chapter puts The Connector Effect to work for you and increases the referrals you give and receive.

Unfortunately, some referrals will go wrong. The customer's problem doesn't get solved, it takes too long or it costs more than was expected. On your own, once you pass a referral you have no way to resolve the issue. Within BNI there's a structure to help problems like these get resolved easily and productively for everyone involved. You've got help within your Chapter to ensure you continue to look like a hero well after you've made a referral.

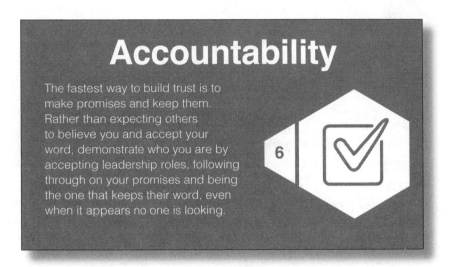

Accountability

The fastest way to build trust is to make promises and keep them. Rather than expecting others to believe you and accept your word, demonstrate who you are by accepting leadership roles, following through on your promises and being the one that keeps their word, even when it appears no one is looking.

6

Without the structure of your BNI Chapter, there's more risk in making a referral. It's more likely you'll give up on becoming a Master Connector rather than continuing to assume that risk every day.

Richard Singery ran out of clients and was about to go bankrupt before he discovered and joined a BNI Chapter in South Africa. Through BNI he rescued his landscaping/irrigation design and installation business, turning it around within six months. When he joined, he had only $156 left in his bank account—he was on thin ice and close to closing his business. With the help of his BNI Chapter, he turned that $156 into $60,000 in less than five months after joining BNI. Three years later he was able to buy his first deep-sea fishing boat and now owns two boats and an off-road truck, and is able to afford plenty of personal travel.

"I'll network online so I don't have to go to meetings."

In a recent survey of 3,400 businesspeople from around the world, social media savvy was ranked dead last in importance as an indicator of great networking ability. Do you think that only applies to old people? The under 30-year-old respondents ranked social media savvy next to last in importance.

Social media can become a valuable source of customers. There are many BNI Members who can help you attract customers via social media.

Becoming a Master Connector with real relationships first will make everything you do on social media more powerful.

Within your BNI Chapter you will be in a competitor-free network that's engineered to help you grow your business. Track the progress of your business growth using closed business as your metric.

After spending a "great deal of effort working the connections on LinkedIn," Karen Nutter, a business coach in the United States, discovered, "with BNI it is SO much easier!"

Karen joined BNI at a time when her business needed growth. In her first year as a Member, her business grew 35%, and then the second year it grew 40%. And every year since she joined, she has generated 30% of her business from her BNI Chapter.

Plus, Karen's BNI Chapter has helped her become a Master Connector. She has discovered that her contacts, friends and family enjoy doing business with her BNI Chapter Members because they show up on time, do a great job and are very polite.

You'll grow your business a lot faster with an effective networking system instead of just using social media.

"But I've been to networking events before; it was a waste of time."

Yes, we have, too. That's why we created the BNI system. Too many people trying to promote their events slap the networking tag on them without providing an environment for real connections to occur.

Too many people use networking as a face-to-face cold-calling approach. These people walk from person to person, focused on selling their products or services.

BNI was carefully created, proven and improved over several decades to generate the greatest possible referrals for you with the smallest time investment.

BNI was carefully created, proven and improved over several decades to generate the greatest possible referrals for you with the smallest time investment.

The Connector Effect is based on relationships. Each new relationship doubles the power of your network. That's why a business card or a handshake at some event gives you so little return on investment. There's no relationship there.

Wendy Prosser did a lot of networking in many different groups to get clients for her virtual personal assistant business headquartered in the United Kingdom. "The results were nowhere near as good as the ones I have had since joining BNI."

As a BNI Member, Wendy is able to focus more time on helping her clients, as 90% of her new clients come from BNI referrals. "There is plenty of support within my Chapter to help me grow," Wendy reports.

There are hundreds of reasons why BNI Chapters are so effective in growing your business. Three big ones are that at each meeting, there is a room full of Givers, a community that encourages referrals and an agenda that focuses attention on the primary purpose of the meeting, which is growing your business.

Within your BNI Chapter there's a system that's been perfected over several decades to create meaningful relationships for you. This environment is designed to get you the referrals that will best grow your business. This won't happen by chance. And you won't find these opportunities at those cocktail party events.

"BNI Members are not my target market."

It's not the people in the room. It's who the people in the room know. And you never know who they know.

For some businesses, the Members around the table could be prospective customers for them. For you, if those aren't your target customer, those people know people who could be your customer.

Many Chapters will conduct an exercise asking each Member to come to the meeting with the name of a specific person who would be a great referral for them.

It's remarkable how many times someone in the Chapter is related to that person, is an old college buddy or is a current or former client of that person.

BNI Membership is not about the people in the room being your customer. It's about who they know who will become your next customer.

BNI Membership is not about the people in the room being your customer. It's about who they know who will become your next customer.

And even more important than that, you have the opportunity to pass referrals to your Chapter. By giving thoughtful referrals, you become a Master Connector and become the respected problem solver within your community.

Because of huge competitors with large advertising budgets, advertising wasn't generating enough customers for Edwin Duria to survive. Edwin is a Filipino living in the United Arab Emirates. He is the Founder and Managing Director of PLAY Middle East Business Consultancy.

BNI helped transform Edwin from being an employee to a business owner. It has opened a lot of important doors for him. Today he's closing approximately 80% of the referrals he generates from his BNI Chapter.

And the best part is that Edwin reports being a part of his BNI Chapter has helped him be a better person, have more friends and certainly grow his business.

The 47 members of his Chapter form the most diverse BNI Chapter within the UAE, with members from 26 different nationalities.

When you become a Master Connector by joining a BNI Chapter, attend your Weekly Meetings to build relationships and put Givers Gain® into motion by passing referrals, you'll generate valuable referrals from your BNI Chapter in return. Once you put The Connector Effect to work, you never know who is within those connections.

"I have prospect lists to market to already."

When we launched the first BNI Chapter in 1985, direct mail marketing was at the height of its popularity. Direct mail involves sending a thousand people a piece of mail hoping you'll get 20 new customers. Few small businesses can afford the design, printing and postage costs to get such a small return. This is especially true when it stops working.

After direct marketing came cold calling, which also became popular with businesspeople. It involves the same idea but a different device. A businessperson will pick up the phone to call 100 people, get rejected 98 times, but get two new buyers. And making cold calls takes a whole lot more time than a 90-minute BNI Chapter meeting once a week.

And today there's spam email. And some online social networks are promoted as a panacea for cold approach messages because they target "just the right prospects."

Cold marketing approaches turn you into a pest that's begging for attention rather than the respected business leader that the highest value customers seek out when they have a problem.

Referred customers spend more, are more loyal and will refer other quality new customers to you.

Instead, you have the opportunity to work with prospects who call you ready to do business because they've been referred to you. Referred customers spend more, are more loyal and will refer other quality new customers to you. There's not a more fun, fast and effective marketing approach than becoming a Master Connector within your local BNI Chapter.

After relocating from the Netherlands to Germany with her family, Emmie Veltmaat wanted to realize her dream and share her taste of specialty tea with other people. Brand new to the country, she opened a tea store to ensure the enjoyment of fine tea was accessible to everyone. However, within just three months it appeared her plan was a complete failure.

Cold calling wasn't bringing her any new clients. She considered returning to the Netherlands as there initially didn't appear to be a market for her products in Germany. Then, one of her customers invited her to visit the local BNI Chapter.

She received referrals at her first meeting. And although she was accepted to the Chapter, the membership fee was a problem, even though it was pretty nominal compared with the opportunities it would later provide. But with some encouragement from her

Chapter Members, she overcame it and has never regretted it.

Everything changed in a short time. Now Emmie receives 50% of her business from her BNI Chapter. She has met a lot of great people who support her company and has been able to pursue personal development at the same time. BNI has been more successful and gratifying than the failure and rejection she faced getting customers from cold calling.

Emmie has used her BNI Chapter to become a Master Connector. She's able to help her clients by giving recommendations to so many professional services. Plus, she says, "Without BNI, I would not have managed to grow my business the way it's possible now."

Paolo Coirazza, a public accountant/auditor from Canada, used to print thousands of advertising circulars to distribute through the Canada Post in the hope that he'd get some clients during the income tax period. However, the printing and postage costs exceeded the business he generated.

He was such a shy person when he joined BNI that getting people to take action was quite a challenge. When he delivered the tax return to his first client he received as a referral from his BNI Chapter, the client broke down in tears and started hugging him. He'd just told her that she'd receive a tax refund instead of owing more taxes. She was his first testimonial; when word spread, Paolo was able to generate the referrals he needed to grow his business.

Building Relationships

No one is successful on their own. Becoming good at developing relationships, creating a support network and always growing your network are the keys to success in business and in life.

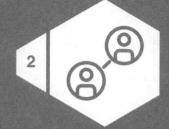

It may feel noble to try to win in business by doing everything yourself. You may feel as though it'll make you truly independent. However, becoming a Master Connector gives you more independence and success than trying to do it all by yourself.

In the several decades since we founded BNI, we have discovered that there is a shortcut. Next, we'll outline the single fastest way to become a Master Connector and grow your business through your BNI Chapter.

Chapter 4
Secrets to Becoming a Master Connector

Before he discovered becoming a Master Connector through his BNI Chapter, Graham Lockett, who owns a digital marketing business in New Zealand, was about to give up. He'd been in business for four years, cold calling 40 people a day and absolutely hating it. Giving up and taking a sales role at a massive corporation looked like his best option. He could barely pay the bills.

He only had a small bit of money left in his bank account. He thought about throwing it into an advertising campaign as a last-ditch effort. Then a client of his encouraged him to attend a local BNI Chapter.

Graham had never been good at networking. Plus, he had only been comfortable in social situations where he already knew everyone present. BNI sounded like the opposite of where he wanted to be.

Now, just one year later, he's able to enjoy operating his company and living life on his own terms. He has generated $21,000 in one year as a proud BNI Member.

"The things that have changed in my business life are massive. I have learnt to be more accountable and hold myself to a higher standard of work," Graham reports. "I am much more responsible because I can't betray my fellow Member when they refer work to me."

Traditions + Innovation

Traditions tell us who we are. Innovation tells us where we want to go. You need to know who you are as an organization, and you need to know where you are going as an organization. This keeps you from losing your place in the world while you continue to strive to create a better life for yourself and others.

4

Your passion and work ethic mean you are already great at your business or profession. That's your foundation. Becoming a Master Connector is the innovation that'll help you generate new customers. Spend less time and money getting new clients so you have more time to do the work you enjoy.

Business is a journey, not a destination. Your business can give you financial freedom as well as control over your time, but only when you've created a dependable method of generating new and high-quality customers.

And no matter how successful you become, it's critical that you continue to learn about your craft and about how to build the trust of employees, referral partners and customers.

Over the next several chapters we are going to outline a new way to conduct business. While there are hundreds of thousands of BNI Members throughout the world today, few of them were good at being a Master Connector before they joined BNI. And no one expects you to do everything perfectly in your first year or two, either. (Note that there is not any ONE perfect way within BNI. Every Member brings their own style and unique experience.)

Our goal is to make it as easy as possible for you to become a Master Connector so you can put The Connector Effect™ to work for your business. Your business life will be a lot more lucrative, fun and empowering that way. Master Connectors find it easier to build trust with strangers. You can solve problems by passing referrals.

What you discover will help you grow a successful business whether you belong to a BNI Chapter or not. That said, we think you'll find that it's a lot easier to become a successful Master Connector once you've joined BNI.

Your BNI Chapter puts you into a room full of "givers" who are dedicated to helping you and your business grow.

And most important, your BNI Chapter puts you into a room full of "givers" who are dedicated to helping you and your business grow.

Within the first three chapters we've revealed that becoming a Master Connector is the fastest way to grow your business. Over the remaining chapters we are going to show you step-by-step the fastest way for you to become a Master Connector. Here are the critical lessons you'll discover in the next few chapters:

Chapter 5 – Growing Your Business by Attracting the Customers You Deserve

Your customers are bombarded by thousands of marketing messages each day; they ignore 99% of them. You'll discover how to craft your message to break through the clutter so you get heard and you attract the customers you deserve.

Chapter 6 – Building Relationships That Turn Into a Consistent Referral Flow

You are going to attend a lot of meetings in your life. Most businesspeople "wing it," meaning little-to-no prep and a lot of time wasted chatting when they could, instead, be building meaningful relationships.

Chapter 7 – Be the One Who Gets All the Referrals

It always seems like one or two people get most of the referrals while everyone else battles for scraps. You can become the person who gets the referrals in your field when you become a Master Connector.

Chapter 8 – How to Get More High-Value Referral Customers

Referral customers spend more with you and remain loyal for a longer period of time than customers from other marketing methods. You increase the number of referrals you generate for your business each time your network grows.

Chapter 9 – Maximizing Your Referrals by Increasing Your Visibility

You never receive referrals from someone who doesn't know, like and trust you. Becoming known, growing relationships and becoming trusted always begins with being visible. You've got to show up before you can stand out.

Chapter 10 – Accelerating the Positive Impact to Your Business and Life

Discover opportunities to grow your experience and network in order to generate referrals. This will make it easier for you to seek other career opportunities, community board service positions and other interesting and lucrative ventures.

Chapter 11 – Generate More Referrals in the Least Amount of Time

You'll find that it has never been as easy, fun or efficient to grow your business as it is when you begin tapping into these proven Master Connector systems. You benefit from the lessons learned from several decades of innovations by Master Connectors around the world.

All this may feel overwhelming at first. It can feel strange anytime you learn something new. Remember, the shortcut is always the least-traveled path. But we'll be with you every step of the way to help you succeed.

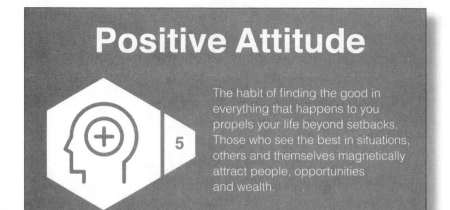

In fact, if you focus one full day on learning the skills within each chapter, you will be on your way to becoming a Master Connector.

Just like learning golf, tennis or swimming, you can always improve. But the secrets you'll discover within the next few chapters will help you get pro-level results even if you are new to networking or never thought you'd be interested in meeting new people.

And the more experience you bring, the easier it'll be for you to get better results. Now, time is money, so let's get started.

Chapter 5
Growing Your Business by Attracting the Customers You Deserve

Even though Vasim Sheikh had attended many other types of networking groups in the past, his first introduction to the 30 members within his BNI Chapter was "an eye-opener." People were actually curious to learn about his business and started connecting him to their contacts. It was so different from other events where people were only interested in promoting their own business to find customers for themselves.

After completing his M.B.A., Vasim wanted to start a business with his life partner. They chose to become event planners, to take over the logistics for people doing events.

Each week, every BNI Member gets to give their Weekly Presentation. This gives each Member the opportunity to brief the Chapter on their business and the perfect customers for that business. It also allows each Member to tell their client success stories.

This is one of Vasim's favorite parts of his BNI Membership. Between the training BNI offers and the weekly practice, he has become a lot better. He knows a lot more about how to explain his business in a compelling way. Plus, he learned how to tell his success stories in a really effective way so he gets more clients.

In fact, within his first month he generated five referrals from his BNI Chapter.

Being able to tell your story in an effective way is crucial to growing your business, whether you become a Master Connector or not. In the last several decades we've trained millions of business leaders how to craft a concise and compelling sales story. By learning this, you'll be able to tell your story briefly but effectively. And when you do, customers will pay attention, referral sources will understand who to refer to you and you'll get more of the customers you deserve.

Your customers are bombarded by thousands of marketing messages each day; they ignore 99% of them. You'll discover how to craft your message to break through the clutter so you get heard and you attract the customers you deserve.

Most businesspeople make the mistake of explaining what they do. They talk about their product or the services they provide.

People don't care what you do; they only care what they are left with after you do what you do.

People don't care what you do; they only care what they are left with after you do what you do.

For instance, when describing BNI we don't talk about the structured meetings, the breadth of training, the sophisticated technology BNI provides or anything else. Instead, we focus on the after: "BNI helps people create referrals for life."

What are your customers left with after you deliver your product or service?

By working with millions of business leaders through the years, we've learned that there's a specific language that sells. Plus, when you use this language you won't look "sales-y" or sound pushy.

Once you've mastered these easy steps, you'll be able to enhance and align all of your marketing material to make it more effective. And your message will begin to spread throughout your network both within and outside BNI.

Once you learn the system, use it to create your winning message and practice delivering it, you'll be able to:

- Deliver powerful Weekly Presentations within your BNI Chapter meeting;
- Update your website and online marketing materials to clarify your unique message;
- Make all of the marketing and advertising you create more effective;
- Generate more referrals within BNI and word-of-mouth marketing outside of it; and
- Transform people you meet into active participants in your referral network.

3 Simple Steps to Grow Your Business by Attracting the Customers You Deserve

Review the steps below. Within one or two minutes write down the answer to each of these questions. Don't overthink each question or spend a long time writing. Just jot down the first two or three sentences that come to mind.

Step 1: Describe Your Best Target Customer.

Many would-be marketers fail because they never define a target customer. Instead they use words like "everybody" or "anybody." Defining a target market is never limiting; rather, it gives referral partners a mental picture of the best customer to refer to you. In BNI, we frequently say "Specific is Terrific"—the more specific you are, the more referrals you will receive.

Answer these questions if your customers are consumers:

1. Think of a person who is already a great customer for you.

2. In what area do they live?

3. What is their family status and profession?

4. How does their household income compare with the average?

5. What are they planning, proud of or unhappy about?

Now repeat steps 2-5 thinking about two or three other great customers you have.

If your customers are other businesses, answer these questions:

1. Think of a business that is already a great customer for you.

2. What line of business is that customer in?

3. What's the approximate size of that business?

4. Who within that business makes the buying decisions for your product or service?

5. What are their primary goals, or what's the problem they are trying to solve when buying your product?

Repeat steps 2-5 thinking about two or three other great customers you have.

The key to this section is to be specific. By being specific you are serving your Chapter best by giving them a clear idea of who your target customer is. The more specific you are, the more effective they will be in finding those referrals for you.

Step 2: What Are the Problems You Solve for Your Target Customer?

All businesses exist to solve a problem. Too many businesspeople talk about their products and services. This sounds self-serving, and it pushes people away. In actuality, talking about the problems you solve makes you into a Giver who attracts customers.

1. List at least three problems your best customer has that make them ideal for your business.

2. What is the worst thing that can possibly happen to your customer if their problem isn't solved?

3. What is the best thing that can happen to your customer once their problem is solved?

4. Do you have any evidence or client success stories to illustrate how you help your customers?

(We call these customer stories "client testimonials." Client testimonials are a great way to give your BNI Chapter a clear idea of what exactly you deliver and the best person to refer to you. Plus, they demonstrate that your Chapter Members can trust you to consistently deliver what you promise.)

Step 3: Build Your Presentation.

Now let's pull the information you wrote in steps 1 and 2 above into a brief presentation.

Here are the five elements of the perfect business introduction:

1. Introduce yourself: Provide your name and company name.

2. State your professional classification.

3. Tell a brief story about a problem you solved for a customer.

4. Request a referral—who do you know who is [insert target customer] who suffers from the problem of [#1 problem you solve].

5. Repeat your name and company name.

Each week, tell a different story or show how you solved a different problem. Over time you are training your referral partners on all of the reasons to refer you.

Each week, tell a different story or show how you solved a different problem. Over time you are training your referral partners on all of the reasons to refer you.

The business owner with the clear message is the one who attracts the most customers. Too many marketers complicate their message by talking too much about themselves. We help you focus on a few simple elements to create a powerful marketing message.

Once you learn how to create these presentations for your business, you can use this skill for any club, charity or campaign you lead. And you can be the person who helps to make it into a success.

As a new BNI Member you'll have the opportunity to deliver your Weekly Presentation in a competitor-free environment, to a room full of business leaders practicing Givers Gain®. That's a powerful advantage over your competition.

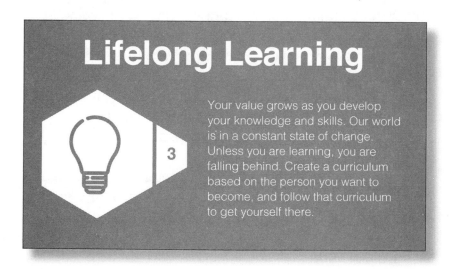

Lifelong Learning

3

Your value grows as you develop your knowledge and skills. Our world is in a constant state of change. Unless you are learning, you are falling behind. Create a curriculum based on the person you want to become, and follow that curriculum to get yourself there.

Universities around the world hand out diplomas
in business and marketing without ever teaching
networking.

Universities around the world hand out diplomas in
business and marketing without ever teaching networking.

Dr. Lupita Cruz, a dentist in Mexico, recently said,
"Dental school taught me everything I needed to know—
after someone was sitting in the dental chair with their
mouth wide open in front of me. What dental school did
not teach me was how to get a patient into that chair!"
As a Master Connector within her BNI Chapter, she has
learned how to get patients into the chair.

For businesspeople, it's crucial that you continue
acquiring the skills that you need to actually grow your
business—not just the skills to serve existing clients.

Most businesspeople can't deliver an effective,
short presentation describing how they help their
customers. This is the first step of networking—being
able to explain what you do in a way that helps your
target customers clearly see a picture within their mind.

That's why we provide a template as the structure
for creating a great presentation. This template even
works for introverts! Or should we say, especially for
introverts.

Every workday there are thousands of introverts in
BNI Chapters around the world giving their brief Weekly
Presentations. When you see everyone else in your
Chapter giving their presentation, you'll see that it's not
so hard. And you may discover that you are better at

speaking than you thought. No matter how good you are at presenting your story when you start, within a short time you'll amaze yourself at how good you become.

As a BNI Member, you'll be able to practice your presentation each week. As your confidence grows, you'll want to create and deliver new Weekly Presentations. Perhaps you can share new customer stories, more specific profiles and unique problems you've solved for your customers recently. This way your BNI Chapter gets to know you and your ideal customer really well so they can pass you higher and higher quality referrals.

Consider this example: Ruth May of Waterfall Nail & Beauty in South Africa had always been a very nervous public speaker. At her first BNI meeting, she was a bit daunted by the prospect of speaking in front of other business leaders she had only just met. However, she could see the structure was well thought out, and she was impressed with the referrals that were given in the room *that day*.

Although she still "prefers to be on the sidelines," her BNI Chapter has helped her develop impressive public speaking skills. In fact, she's now comfortable and able to speak freely during her Weekly Presentations and to articulate her thoughts well.

Before BNI, Ruth was able to get the clients she needed by doing a great job; she gained new clients through word of mouth. But times changed when four other salons opened up on the same road. That's when the power of BNI really came into play. Today, BNI is her main source of marketing and new clients.

That's not all: Ruth has become a Master Connector. Her circle of influence has grown, and her friends and customers call her when they need an electrician, lawyer, financial advisor or any other service provider. She has found it easy to refer her fellow BNI Members because she's used most of them herself and very much trusts their work.

While she has been a BNI Member for seven years, she's been in a managerial position for four years. She now gets to work on her business rather than in it. And through her Chapter, she's engaged a graphic designer to help her brand her business, as well as someone to help her with Facebook and Instagram marketing. She has even engaged a business coach who has helped her create the systems she needs to really scale her business.

BNI first helped Ruth become a Master Connecter to grow her influence within her community, and then it helped her develop her primary new customer engagement system, and then it helped her to get the resources she needed to become the manager of her business rather than working on nails herself.

Chapter 6
Building Relationships That Turn Into a Consistent Referral Flow

When his service with the U.S. Army ended, Gary Bulson was looking for work. He answered an ad in a local newspaper for a company that was looking to hire movers. This started Gary's long journey with his boss, who became his partner until he bought him out completely.

For years, Men on the Move, a moving and storage company, attracted most of their customers through word of mouth from past customers. Plus, they invested in Yellow Pages advertising and Angie's List while networking at the Jaycees and their local Chamber of Commerce.

He knew about BNI for quite some time. However, he didn't feel like he could attend Weekly Meetings because of the day-to-day obligations of running his business. He also wondered about the expense. With the time and money, Gary wondered if joining his local BNI Chapter could really be worth it. But after attending a BNI Visitor's Day event, everyone was so friendly, nice and helpful, he joined BNI so he could get to know them better.

Within three months of joining, he received referrals for new jobs valued at more than $8,000. Plus, Gary says, "I've found a sales staff of some great businesspeople (fellow BNI Members) who are respected in their fields and who refer us to others. If I had known

10 years ago what I know now, I would've joined back then. WORTH EVERY PENNY!"

Most of all, Gary discovered the power of The Connector Effect™. He reports, "It helps strengthen the relationships with my family, friends and customers because I am a resource for them."

While Gary loves the growth of his business, what he enjoys the most are the One-to-Ones. These are meetings where Gary meets with one other Member of his BNI Chapter individually and outside of the meeting. And his goal is to complete three or four One-to-Ones each month.

"While the Chapter meetings are great, it's the One-to-One meetings where you get to know each other and build that trust bond," says Gary. "Once you do One-to-Ones, Chapter meetings are even more productive and fun to attend. It's something I look forward to."

Remember, you are going to attend a lot of business meetings in your life. Most businesspeople "wing it," meaning little-to-no preparation and a lot of time wasted chatting when they could be building meaningful relationships.

Since 1985, BNI has been teaching businesspeople how to turn One-to-One meetings into productive network-building opportunities. When following this approach, any One-to-One meeting could lead to an immediate referral. More important, when you follow these steps, they turn a One-to-One meeting attendee into a valuable, long-term member of your referral network.

BNI's data has proven that those who do three or more One-to-One meetings each month give and receive twice as many referrals as those who do one or fewer One-to-Ones. This is according to research by Beatrice Sparacino as part of her thesis at the School of Management at Bocconi University in Milan, Italy. She analyzed BNI Chapter records and compared the number of referrals generated by BNI Members to the number of One-to-One meetings.

Once you've mastered these easy steps, you'll be able to:

- Build relationships with the right people who can pass you business immediately, and for years to come;

- Turn strangers into friends who are trained to look for customers who are a good fit for you and who are motivated to connect you with them;

- Get more strong contacts from every networking event you attend because you finally know how to follow up to make yourself stand out and be memorable;

- Generate more referrals within BNI and referral marketing outside of it; and

- Make every business meeting more productive because you have a system to turn strangers into referral partners that know, like and trust you.

The Connector Effect is based upon relationships. You create relationships by identifying points of shared interests.

The Connector Effect is based upon relationships. You create relationships by identifying points of shared interests.

BNI's structure for One-to-One meetings is designed to help you identify mutual interests. Even among people who may not appear on the surface to be alike. By connecting both personal interests as well as business interests, you'll be able to form a stronger relationship. And each relationship increases the impact of The Connector Effect in your life.

Here are the essential steps of BNI's *GAINS Exchange* for productive One-to-One meetings.

Goals:

Ask about their financial, professional, educational and personal objectives they want or need to meet for themselves and for people who are important to them. A great way to develop a relationship is by helping someone achieve something that's important to them. Consider if there's anyone in your network who you could help move closer to achieving their most important goals.

Accomplishments:

Some of your best insights into others come from knowing what goals they have achieved, what projects they've completed and who they've worked with in the past. Consider whether anyone in your network could benefit by connecting with a person with these accomplishments.

Interests:

Your interests—the things you enjoy doing, talking about,

listening to or collecting—can help you meaningfully connect with others. People are more willing to spend time with those who share their interests or know something important about them. Ask about their interests, and consider others in your network with similar interests.

Networks:

A network can be an institution, company, civic organization, religious organization or professional association. Ask about the networks they participate in. Consider who you know within your network that would benefit from knowing someone within those networks.

Skills:

The more you know about the talents, abilities and assets of the people in your network, the better equipped you are to find competent and reliable services when you or someone you know needs help.

Your fellow BNI Members will know to reciprocate by asking these questions of you and following up with any referral opportunities they have. While you can make any One-to-One meeting more productive using this process, you'll always get the best results with your fellow BNI Members.

You'll find a *GAINS Exchange Profile* form on page 148 of this book. BNI Members can access a full-size version of this form within the BNI Member Success Training Program.

Prepare for your first One-to-Ones by taking a few minutes to complete the second column of this form with your answers to the GAINS Exchange. This way you'll be well prepared ahead of time to share your Goals,

Accomplishments, Interests, Networks and Skills. And if you have this form with you, use the third column to write down the GAINS of your One-to-One partner. Taking notes demonstrates that you value the new relationship you are forming with your One-to-One partner. Be sure to keep your notes and refer back to them periodically (e.g., once per quarter) to continue building your relationships.

Turning Contacts Into Connections

Especially when you are starting out, you'll have plenty of Members within your BNI Chapter with whom to do initial One-to-Ones. But you are always going to meet new people throughout your week. And even though you are a Master Connector generating referrals from your Chapter to grow your business, it's important to improve your networking skills in other settings.

We recommend *Networking Like a Pro: Turning Contacts Into Connections*, co-authored by a co-author of this book and BNI Founder & Chief Visionary Officer, Dr. Ivan Misner. One of the essential lessons in this book is following up.

After you complete One-to-Ones, look for ways to follow up. Remember, The Connector Effect increases the value of your entire referral network with each relationship. The stronger your relationships, the bigger you'll benefit from The Connector Effect.

Here are several follow-up ideas from *Networking Like a Pro*:

Send a thank you card – Especially in the age of digital communications, a handwritten thank you card makes a great impression.

Send a small but thoughtful gift – This can be a small, inexpensive gift. Perhaps something from within your industry. This can be a powerful relationship builder that can increase referrals you receive. But of course, do this for the relationship building—not as some kind of quid pro quo.

Set up a brief social activity – Whenever you discover shared interests, consider following up with a brief social activity. It always builds relationships, and it's fun!

Make a thoughtful referral – Passing a referral is a great way to build a relationship when it's a good fit.

Send an article of interest – Pass along articles you discover that would be interesting. This signals to the other person that you know them well and are investing in building your relationship with them.

Each of these follow-up strategies will help augment the relationship-building impact of your One-to-One meetings. And there's a lot more in the book *Networking Like a Pro.*

Businesspeople who know how to build personal relationships quickly will reap the benefits of consistent, long-term referral relationships and will build the most wonderful, professional relationships of their lives.

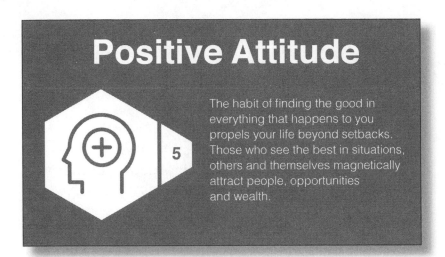

Positive Attitude

The habit of finding the good in everything that happens to you propels your life beyond setbacks. Those who see the best in situations, others and themselves magnetically attract people, opportunities and wealth.

One of the many benefits of BNI is the opportunity to practice One-to-One meetings with your Chapter. This puts you into a supportive environment where you become better and better at answering these questions. Plus, you'll become better at active listening so you can connect to build a relationship.

Whenever we start talking about ourselves, it's easy to keep talking. And talking. And talking. And so on. Outside of BNI, it's so rare for people to really ask us questions beyond what we thought of the local sporting event or the weather. Being an active listener encourages others to keep talking, sharing their story and building your mutual relationship.

Your BNI Chapter understands and applauds when this happens. When you catch yourself talking too long, though, finish your thought and then turn the conversation back to the GAINS Exchange by asking the next question. The best One-to-Ones alternate the focus of the conversation between the individuals to ensure equal involvement of both parties.

There will also be times when your One-to-One partner begins to take over the conversation. Time slips by without giving you the opportunity to tell them about your GAINS Profile. When that happens, allow them to finish their thought and say, "Wow, that's great. Thank you for sharing that with me. How about we get back to the GAINS Exchange?"

It's human to digress, especially when you and your partner are active listeners and you're both passionate about the topic. Within BNI, this is our polite way of redirecting the conversation to get back to the agenda.

BNI's structure produces the best possible results in the least amount of time. It's there to help you be more productive, efficient and professional, both inside of your Chapter meetings and throughout your week.

You'll discover that most BNI Members stay on task. BNI's structure produces the best possible results in the least amount of time. It's there to help you be more productive, efficient and professional, both inside of your Chapter meetings and throughout your week.

"One-to-Ones give two BNI Members time to focus on each other to gain valuable information about the person and the business so we can pass quality referrals to each other," says Amanda Kell-Scobie, owner of a senior in-home care business in the United States. "Without One-to-Ones, everyone would get busy in their lives and not make time to focus on the aspects that will boost business referrals, not just at the weekly meeting."

Amanda has been a caregiver since she was 17 years old. After working for someone else for 10 years, she decided to start her own elder care company.

When she launched her business, she needed insurance. Her insurance agent asked her, "How are you going to get new business?" He connected her with his BNI Chapter.

She attended the Chapter meeting the next morning. However, because she's an introvert, it took her some time to become acclimated. Within minutes, though, everyone made her feel welcome. She naturally started feeling comfortable and was able to connect within about an hour. Amanda made the decision to join BNI right away.

"BNI has played an integral role in the success and growth of my business," Amanda reports. "BNI gives me the tools I need to not only be a better public speaker but a better businessperson overall. I have also learned how to get my point across in 30 seconds or less!"

Through your BNI experience, you'll learn a lot of skills. So far we've told you about Weekly Presentations and One-to-Ones. While these are important for your participation in BNI, they are also critical for you to learn as a businessperson.

As you practice your Weekly Presentations, you'll be inspired to review the questions in Chapter 5 more deeply. You'll refine your presentation. Maybe you'll also create different variations to keep it fresh each week. As you do, you'll discover ways to improve every sales message within your company. Your ads will perform better, your website will improve and you'll close more sales.

While you are doing three or four One-to-Ones each month, you'll get to practice creating strong relationships with other businesspeople in your community. This grows your network and referral base now while improving your skill at connecting with customers, prospects and even family.

BNI was created in 1985. Many Members have stayed for decades because of the relationships and skills they've developed within the network.

These skills can be life changing. In the next chapter we'll reveal the single most important skill a Master Connector can develop. It's a skill you'll be improving upon for the rest of your business life.

Chapter 7

Be the One Who Gets All the Referrals

"99.9% of my work comes from BNI," says Silvano Coan of South Africa. In two years, he grew his debt collection business from its initial launch to a profitable three-person operation.

> "99.9% of my work
> comes from BNI."

Even better, he did this without a website. He invested zero dollars in advertising. Instead, he got to keep that money because he grew his business by becoming a Master Connector.

"Being a BNI Member is an unfair advantage over all other businesses," admits Silvano. "I have 33 trained salespeople within my Chapter."

Silvano had been doing debt collection for a law firm for 12 years. It all changed when two different BNI Members gave him the same idea, three days apart. Why not do account management? Why not take over the job of collections immediately after your client sends out the invoice rather than waiting until the debt is past due months later?

As soon as Silvano joined, he embraced the Givers Gain® philosophy by passing referrals to his Chapter

Members. He says, "The more connections you make and the more you help your fellow members, without expecting anything in return, the faster karma will sort you out."

Today, Silvano's only regret is that he didn't put in more work passing referrals to other BNI Members during his first year. "The return on investment of time is absolutely phenomenal," he says.

Have you ever wondered why some people generate the majority of the referrals in a market and get all the good customers? It always seems like one or two people get most of the referrals while everyone else battles for the scraps. You can become the person who gets the referrals in your field when you become a Master Connector.

Master Connectors don't promote themselves, talk about their accomplishments or say "I," other than to say, "I'd like you to meet … ." You'll often find them with at least two other people around them, speaking with both at the same time. They focus on building or deepening relationships between the other two people. Forging and fostering connections for others more than for themselves.

The single most important skill in business is the ability to create business relationships between two people, based on core values and mutual interests.

Since 1985, BNI has been teaching professionals like you to grow their businesses by building relationships between other people. It's the foundation of Givers Gain and is the fastest way for you to become the most successful person in your field. Once you learn this system, you'll:

- Double the growth of your referral network as each connection you make creates two people who appreciate you and want to pass referrals to you;

- Generate more referrals for your own business as your referral network expands;

- Turn any new referral you get into network growth opportunities as you make additional non-competitive referrals for your new customers;

- Generate more referrals from within BNI as well as within your entire referral network; and

- Grow your business to dominate your market by generating positive word-of-mouth advertising.

Your BNI Chapter gives you a network you can trust to whom you can refer your friends, family and best customers. Each BNI Chapter is a group of businesspeople you trust to consistently do what they promise. And because they trust you to do the same, they will pass referrals of their friends, family and customers to you in kind.

Making strong referral connections is the fastest way to grow your business today. But you've got to do it in the right way to maximize your impact.

The stronger the connections you make,
the bigger the impact you'll have.

The stronger the connections you make, the bigger the impact you'll have.

One of the biggest mistakes people make when giving referrals is to do it too weakly. Most people are afraid to make connections. Everyone has been burned at some point in the past. Maybe you've given a recommendation that turned out badly. It felt bad when you made a connection and things went wrong. Under the circumstances, you risk losing trust rather than gaining it.

It feels safer to give no referrals at all. Or when you do give referrals, you might do it poorly. You might do this by giving out the name along with a warning or a disclaimer like, "This is who I used; not sure if she's right for you."

There are a lot of reasons for this.

First, while you may have had a good experience with a vendor, maybe that vendor didn't see you as a source of future referrals. Being a Master Connector gives you great leverage because businesspeople don't want to lose all the future referrals you can pass them. Thus, they may work harder for you than they would for a stranger off the street.

Next, it's possible that the parties didn't understand why you were making that particular connection. Perhaps there was a misunderstanding of needs and abilities that led to a disappointing outcome.

That's why Master Connectors use a very specific method of passing referrals. It helps prevent misunderstandings and ensures both parties will be on their best behavior because they don't want to let YOU down. This is because you were so thoughtful and intentional with your connection.

Best of all, doing it right costs you nothing. And it earns you everything. When you learn this skill, it's something you can use to build trust and create stronger relationships for the rest of your life!

How to Give Referrals Like a Master Connector

Master Connectors take care to ensure both sides of a referral feel comfortable, connected and engaged. Learn how to move up the referral levels to build the strongest network for your own business.

Here are the five types of referrals; the higher the number the better the referral:

1. Authorize your prospect to use your name to get great service. It sounds like, "Alice is expecting your call; be sure to mention my name."

2. You pass along a letter or email recommendation. This is often done as an email introduction to connect the prospect with the provider they are seeking.

3. Begin to qualify the need of the prospect for the provider's solution and explain how the provider can solve that problem.

4. Qualify and schedule an appointment for the prospect and the member to solidify the when and where for their conversation.

5. Qualify the need and schedule a meeting with yourself, the prospect and the provider so you are there to translate how the connection makes sense.

Master Connectors always strive to make #4 or #5 connections. Different connections are, of course, appropriate for different situations.

Too many networkers focus on volume over quality. When they do pass referrals, they focus on the weaker type #1 and #2 connections. Always start at #5 whenever possible.

Your goal is to create three-legged relationships around you. Whenever possible, create a conversation.

Your goal is to create three-legged relationships around you. Whenever possible, create a conversation. In person is best but an introduction over the phone works as well.

Your introductions should have two levels.

First, mention who each person is, what they do and what they are currently doing. Explain why it's a good idea for these two to meet each other. One way to initiate the referral connection is to say, "Knowing the two of you, it would be worthwhile for you two to speak."

Next (this is far more important), mention what makes each person great at what they do. Explain their core values, interests and skills. This is information you can get from great One-to-One meetings. Your goal is to build the credibility of each party with your introduction.

But what if you just met someone for the first time? How are you supposed to talk about their core values? When you've never done this, it feels difficult. It can feel like you need to spend a lot of time with each person before you can make a connection.

When you try it, you'll be amazed at how quickly you are able to get good at it.

Let's go back to your meeting with Melissa Overton from Chapter 1. You are meeting her for the first time;

how are you supposed to know her values?

By being an active listener while trying to look like you aren't overhearing her phone conversation, you have discovered all you need to know. She's obviously a loyal daughter who is concerned about her dad's well-being. And she's more responsible and attentive than her sibling.

While in her office you could call the appropriate people within your network and introduce her by saying, "I'd like to connect you to Melissa Overton. She's new to town and has been selected as the CEO for her company. She's a loyal daughter who is concerned about her father, who is due to get out of the hospital soon."

Next you'll introduce your fellow BNI Member to Melissa and tell both of them specifically why you are connecting them.

You've just delivered a strong level 5 connection. And it took no more time or effort than writing down phone numbers for Melissa to call. However, it's 50 times more powerful for everyone involved.

The moment they discover that your call probably means a great new customer connection for their business, you'll be amazed who and what they step away from to take your call.

Are you concerned someone won't be available when you call? Just watch. The moment they discover that your call probably means a great new customer connection for their business, you'll be amazed who and what they step away from to take your call.

When Melissa Overton and your fellow Chapter Member speak, your BNI Chapter Member will compliment you and your work. And the stronger referrals you make, the more trust those comments will create for you.

Stronger referrals are better for everyone involved. This includes you!

The Easiest Way to Generate Referral Ideas

Another important point in the story about Melissa Overton is that Master Connectors are always looking for referral opportunities.

When you learn to recognize the language of referrals, you'll suddenly realize there are referral opportunities throughout your day. The language of referrals often begins with: "I can't," "I need," "I want" or "I don't know."

Listen for statements like:

- "I can't get my computer to work."

- "I need customers."

- "I want to lose weight."

- "I don't know how to get rid of this back pain."

It's amazing what you hear when you are listening for it. Even if you feel like this never happens around you, give yourself a week or two and you'll suddenly notice it's happening all the time.

Another helpful way to look for referral opportunities is to listen for signals that someone is planning, proud of or unhappy about something.

Planning - People talk about their plans, the next big holiday, their next big vacation, their next big move or a milestone with their family.

If they are planning a move, maybe they'll need a moving company or a real estate professional. If they are planning a long trip, maybe they need a travel agent or a house sitter.

Proud - We brag about our new home, our new promotion and our kids getting accepted to a school.

If someone's kids are going to a great college, do they need renter's insurance or a car so their child can get around town? With a new promotion, maybe they need a real estate professional for a new home or a financial planner for their investments.

Unhappy - A fair number of people complain daily about their health, their home or wasted time or money on an unnecessary service.

For example, a supplier may say to you, "Why is my computer so slow?" They might need a referral to an IT company. Or a friend might complain about the layout of their kitchen—could that be a referral to the builder or designer in your network?

As an active listener, you are tuned into the frequencies of planning, pride and unhappiness.

When you hear them talking about these things, ask them:

- "What is the problem?"
- "How long have they been dealing with this?"
- "How does it make them feel?"

Then ask, "Are you open to an introduction to someone who can help you?"

When you give great referrals, you are ensuring that both parties appreciate you. With each referral connection, you are creating two people who appreciate you. Both are in a great frame of mind to reciprocate by giving you a referral.

That's what Givers Gain is all about. Each referral you give can turn into two referrals for you, or more!

What's better is, the customers you get from referrals …

1. … are easier to convert;

2. … are open to a faster sales process;

3. … will generally spend more with you;

4. … have a stronger sense of loyalty; and

5. … remain your customers for longer.

Edification Increases The Connector Effect

Whenever you receive a referral, take a few moments to compliment the person who referred you to the prospect. This could be a testimonial about their work, a remark about interests you share or a brief story about what you've seen them accomplish within your BNI Chapter.

For instance, let's say Ivan refers Graham to Robert. As the recipient of the referral, the first thing Graham should ask Robert when they connect is, "How do you know Ivan?"

Before you talk about yourself or your product and before you ask the potential customer about his problem, build a relationship with a point of common interest, the person who made the referral.

After Robert tells Graham about his relationship with Ivan, Graham should tell Robert what an amazing person Ivan is. This builds a common connection between you and the potential customer.

If Graham compliments Ivan when he first meets Robert, it'll help Graham build trust with Robert.

We illustrated the power of edification in the opening story of Melissa Overton in Chapter 1. While you won't need to do as many cold prospecting meetings as a BNI Member, you'll always encounter new people. As a Master Connector, you implemented Givers Gain and helped solve Melissa's problem with her father by referring BNI Members within your network. Then, those Members sang your praises to Melissa.

This is a technique for an advanced Master Connector. However, it can make the difference between a referral who delays making a purchase versus one who is ready to take action.

When you give compliments to Members who have referred you, it affirms the trust those referral partners put in you. It builds relationships, which puts The Connector Effect into action to accelerate the trust-building process.

When you give compliments to Members who have referred you, it affirms the trust those referral partners put in you. It builds relationships, which puts The Connector

Effect™ into action to accelerate the trust-building process.

While you should always work to become better at your craft, you can become a Master Connector, which generates high-value customers with a lot less effort than other marketing approaches.

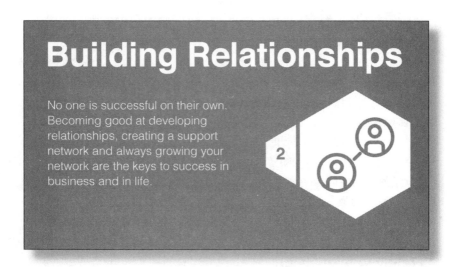

Building Relationships

No one is successful on their own. Becoming good at developing relationships, creating a support network and always growing your network are the keys to success in business and in life.

2

BNI Members around the world have grown hundreds of thousands of different businesses; they've raised money for the charities and movements they are passionate about; and they've even found professionals to solve medical problems for a member of their family, all by being great Master Connectors.

It's the ultimate superpower that's available to you.

Becoming a Master Connector helps you connect with people around the world to solve any problem and tackle any opportunity.

"I have always found that the huge value of BNI is to be able to confidently refer BNI Members to my clients knowing that they will be well cared for," says Kevin Weir, a business coach from the United States. "It's a great feeling to have that in my hip pocket."

Kevin has been a BNI Member for more than 15 years. His BNI Chapter has sent him referrals that have generated several hundred thousand dollars in business for him.

Because BNI gives you the power to give and get referrals, he says, "You'd be crazy not to join a BNI Chapter."

Chapter 8
How to Get More High-Value Referral Customers

Having overspent on advertising, Helen Church was close to closing her property rental and management company in the United Kingdom after just two years in business.

That's when she received an email asking if she was interested in more business. She didn't believe it would work, but her business was failing. She decided to grab her business cards and go to one more meeting as a business owner.

"I was absolutely petrified," Helen admits. "It was a group of nearly 50 Members. Being expected to stand up and speak was nerve-wracking, but I did it." After the meeting Helen was still a bit skeptical, but joined anyway when invited to do so by the Chapter.

That decision was a huge turning point for her. Today, her business has grown to three staff members. It's growing so fast, in fact, she has moved to bigger offices twice. Today, 35% of her clients are BNI Members while another 25% of her clients are from BNI referrals.

"Referrals became my lifeline," explains Helen. "I found the more business I gave out, the more I started to get business back. The relationship building was a turning point in my career."

Business always looks better from the outside than it is from the inside. While it may appear that someone has everything figured out, it could be they are hoping for just the turnaround that BNI Membership could provide.

As a Master Connector, one big problem you can solve for other businesspeople is to give them a system they can use to get new customers and grow their business. This is another example of Givers Gain®: The more guests you invite to your BNI Chapter, the more referrals you will generate as well.

You increase the number of referrals you generate for your business each time your network grows.

BNI Members are trained on how to deliver referrals that turn into business. The more BNI Members in your network, the more high-quality referrals you'll receive. Use your BNI Chapter to help train and motivate businesspeople in your network on how to give you and other Members more referrals.

It's remarkable how a good friend can go years without giving you a referral. Then, when they join BNI, they discover Givers Gain, get trained on how to make referral connections and get excited about passing referrals because of the system in place.

Referred customers spend more with you and remain loyal longer when they become your customer than through any other marketing method.

Plus, referred customers spend more with you and remain loyal longer when they become your customer than through any other marketing method. Inviting guests to Chapter meetings accelerates the number of Master Connectors around you who will pass highly valuable customer referrals to you.

The larger your BNI Chapter, the greater the increase in the number of people within your network who are trained and dedicated to deliver referrals to you. Growing your Chapter allows every member to grow.

Identify the Key Gaps in Your Referral Network

Master Connectors see every role that's missing within their referral network as a lost opportunity to create trust by solving problems. If your network doesn't have a plumber, you can't solve plumbing problems. This is true for yourself and everyone else!

You could fill positions outside of BNI; however, the power of The Connector Effect™ makes it a lot easier to create a comprehensive referral network. The stronger your network, the better Master Connector you can become.

Here are common professional classifications for BNI Members. Each column represents a different contact sphere. BNI's many business categories are organized around contact spheres to better illustrate how many categories share a similar target customer. You'll receive more referrals from businesspeople within your contact sphere because your customers are similar. Businesses within the same contact sphere can share customers more easily.

Sample BNI Business Categories

Events	Marketing Services	Business Services	Real Estate	Trades	Health & Beauty
Photographer Travel Agent Caterer Event Planner	Digital Marketing Graphic Designer Marketing Services Promotional Items	Financial Advisor Accounting Banking Services IT Services	Residential Agent Mortgages P&C Insurance Cleaning Service	Builder Carpentry Painter Electrician	Chiropractor Massage Therapist General Dentist Supplements
Gifts Florist Event Venue Baker	Printer Sign Company Media Services Print Advertising	Commercial Insurance Business Law Telecom Health Insurance	Security Systems Real Estate Law Title Services Inspector	Plumbing Interior Decorator Landscape Services Flooring	Alternative Wellness Cosmetic/Skin Care Fine Jewelry Supplemental Insurance
Wine Merchant Event Marketer DJ/Musician Hotel/Restaurant	Copywriter Videographer Radio Advertising Embroidery	Credit Card Business Advisor Office Machines Employment	Property Management Pest Control Carpet Cleaning Moving Company	Roofing & Gutters Renovations Building Materials Windows/Doors	Clothing/ Accessory Personal Trainer Eye Care Acupuncture

The top row of the chart lists the business categories that are most often represented within BNI Chapters. You'll want to make it a priority to ensure each of these categories is filled first. This grows your BNI Chapter and thus your referral network to more than 24 Members right there. And these are the easiest categories to fill!

The second row lists the next most frequent businesses. Work with your Chapter to ensure these positions are filled. There are another 24 categories right there. Work with your Chapter to set aside time to discuss who knows someone who can fill these positions within your Chapter. Then, make commitments on which Member is going to invite which guest.

Finally, the bottom row gives you another 24 categories for a total of 72 common business types.

Within BNI there are tens of thousands of Members who represent a category that's not within the most common 72. However, these 72 categories give you a great place to start as you work to grow your Chapter, complete your referral network and increase the number of referrals you receive.

Three Simple Steps to Sponsoring New Chapter Members to Grow Your Network

Step 1: Identify

Take an inventory of your current network and identify your incomplete categories. Each one brings you valuable contacts. Make a list of individuals you'd love to have in your network. If you know them, invite them to be your visitor at a Chapter meeting. If you don't know them, ask who within your Chapter is the best person to invite them to grow your network.

Step 2: Invite

The key is to invite your prospective visitor to a meeting.

Within your invite, it's too early to mention areas of commitment, attendance, expectations or cost. Your prospective visitor may make judgments based on that limited information alone. They won't have the benefit of experiencing a Chapter meeting.

Your visitor must come, see a meeting and learn how BNI works before they can make a commitment to joining your network.

Important: Make sure you call or text your guest the night before as a reminder and confirmation to demonstrate their attendance is important to you and to the Chapter.

Step 3: Grow

Make your visitor feel welcome when they arrive. Introduce them to other Members of your Chapter. With each introduction, tell both parties how they could be a beneficial contact. After the meeting, ask your visitor, "How do you feel about applying to join a group of people who are going to pass you business?"

Invite Using the Interview Approach

To help make invitations as simple as possible, here's a sample script you can use:

> Hi, Bob.
>
> I am a member of a network of successful businesspeople who believe in helping each other grow their businesses.
>
> We are interviewing good businesspeople who we can give all of our referrals to. I think you might make a great candidate.
>
> The goal of this meeting is to get to know each other better and to give you an idea of what we are looking for, and then we can decide the best way to move forward from there.
>
> Are you available on [date for next Chapter meeting] to visit with us?

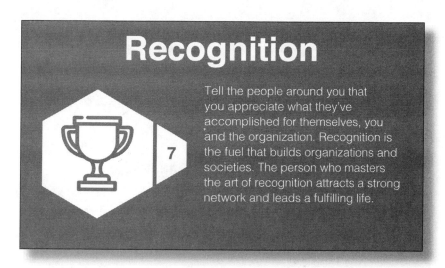

Recognition

Tell the people around you that you appreciate what they've accomplished for themselves, you and the organization. Recognition is the fuel that builds organizations and societies. The person who masters the art of recognition attracts a strong network and leads a fulfilling life.

7

As your Chapter grows, there are more businesspeople focused on passing you valuable referrals. And as you fill your network with professionals within each category, it becomes easier and easier to solve problems for your customers, friends and family by referring them to Members of your Chapter. BNI grows in value as your Chapter grows and you complete your network.

While you are becoming a Master Connector to grow your own business, the way you make it happen is to focus on the needs of those you encounter. Recently an auto mechanic described it this way after sitting through his first BNI Chapter meeting. He's a 30-year veteran in the sales business but sat through the meeting staring into space. When the BNI Executive Director approached him to ask if he could help, the auto mechanic said, "You know this whole networking thing will never work if I am here for myself. I need to take off my bib and put on my apron and learn to serve these people."

Master Connectors are always recognized for serving others. You grow your business through the power of The Connector Effect. Each new relationship increases the effectiveness of your entire network. Focus on building relationships and solving problems for people, and your business will be stronger than ever.

"I consistently invite business colleagues, clients, customers and friends to my BNI Chapter," explains Brian Loebig, a digital marketer in the United States. "It has increased business for Members and has significantly increased my own credibility, trust and standing in the community. I truly think this is why I get so much business from BNI, by connecting people and sharing the amazing opportunity through this organization."

Prior to joining, Brian operated a one-man shop that generated customers through family, friends, Craigslist prospecting, volunteer activities and online lead sources.

In his first year as a member of BNI, he generated about $35,000 in business referrals through his Chapter. That doubled in his second year. And it doubled again in his third year. Today, Brian's business has grown to more than 15 employees generating more than a million dollars in revenue. Brian estimates that between 50-60% of his income is from BNI each year.

Brian has increased his own credibility by becoming a Master Connector. Brian had an instance where he referred a Chapter Member to an acquaintance, and that Chapter Member was able to refer that acquaintance back to him.

It all started when Brian referred his pet groomer to a BNI Member to solve a merchant services problem.

The pet groomer and merchant services provider met and did business together. Plus, while the merchant services provider was meeting with the pet groomer, the pet groomer revealed she needed a new website. The merchant services provider was able to refer the pet groomer back to Brian for web design! The pet groomer wasn't ready to buy web design from Brian until after another BNI Member resolved the merchant services problem.

"The most success came when I decided to take a leadership position within my BNI Chapter and really learn the founding principles," Brian explained. "Since I was starting to get significant business, I wanted to make sure the Chapter utilized all the tools and processes that have been proven to maximize that business!"

As Brian discovered, you have opportunities to generate more visibility by serving in a Chapter Leadership position. There's more on this in Chapter 10. But first, let's talk about how to get more clients as a Master Connector by increasing your visibility.

Chapter 9
Maximizing Your Referrals by Increasing Your Visibility

"I hate public speaking. It makes me nervous!" exclaimed Kymm Mooney, a marketing coordinator at a U.S.-based emergency restoration company with a focus on mold and water. Now she reports that when she speaks in front of a group, "I used to shake and now I don't."

Three years ago, Kymm was in a dead-end retail job. She started with her current company as an office clerk. Now she's the head of marketing. "I never saw this as a path for me. But I'm happy it did become one," she says.

"The turning point for me was being able to turn to our clients and tell them, 'I know someone who can help you, and I trust them,'" Kymm explains. "Customers are in awe when I tell them I have a giant contact sphere of people who can help on the next steps of their project."

Kymm's introduction to BNI came as a substitute attendee for her boss. Her boss was supposed to meet her at the meeting, but his kids got sick. She had to go in blind. "It was a larger group, but they were friendly and welcoming. It was enough to make me want to join a BNI Chapter. I ended up joining the third Chapter I visited. But I look at it as 'finding the dress!' My Chapter was the dress."

Although BNI Members plan to attend every meeting, life happens. Sending a substitute to attend in your place is a great opportunity for your BNI Chapter members, too. They get to add a new person to their network. And it can be a terrific opportunity for your substitute as well.

Kymm's first experience with BNI as a substitute for her boss propelled her career, and she'll never be the same again. Now she's a Master Connector for life!

She says, "The most successful thing that has come from BNI is my confidence in public speaking. I'm an introvert, so stepping out of my comfort zone has never been easy. BNI has helped me do more outside of it, which has helped my business grow and has helped me grow."

You never receive referrals from someone who doesn't know, like and trust you. Becoming known, growing relationships and developing credibility always begins with being visible.

Your BNI Chapter makes a commitment to you by not accepting another member from your professional classification. This enables you to grow your business in an environment free from direct competitors. To maximize the referrals you generate, it's important to be visible at Chapter meetings by attending yourself or ensuring you have someone there to fill in for you.

Visibility helps you grow your referral network and generate referrals that increase your business revenue. When you attend your BNI Chapter meetings, you will:

- Engage your network of businesspeople who know how to generate meaningful referrals to you;

- Build relationships and trust with a room full of Givers dedicated to helping you grow;

- Spark referrals from Chapter Members by delivering your Weekly Presentation;

- Get important solutions to your business challenges rather than having to figure them out on your own; and

- Receive recognition for the referrals you generate, building your reputation with your Chapter's Members.

BNI Chapters That Have the Fewest Absences Close the Most Business

Having an attendance policy ensures you know what to expect from your Chapter Members in exchange for the Chapter's commitment to accept only one Member from each professional classification.

When you send a substitute it's not counted as an absence because you have someone there to represent your business.

This policy serves you by ensuring that when your Chapter commits a business classification to a Member, the Member attends the Chapter meeting so you can pass them referrals. If that Member is not there, Chapter members can't give them referrals. What's worse, they are not able to build relationships or trust. And they're not able to teach fellow Members about the problems they solve for their customers.

While substitutes are welcomed in limited situations, the overuse of substitutes will weaken your relationship with your Chapter, decreasing the referrals you can expect to receive.

Your Chapter's attendance policy protects you from Members who aren't committed to your network. It enables you and your Chapter to fill that position with a business owner who lives the BNI Core Value of Accountability.

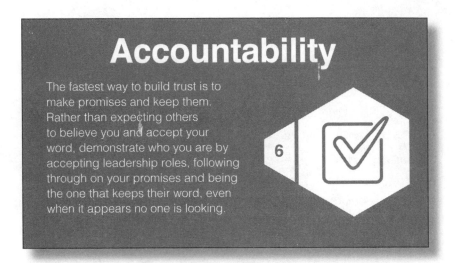

Accountability

The fastest way to build trust is to make promises and keep them. Rather than expecting others to believe you and accept your word, demonstrate who you are by accepting leadership roles, following through on your promises and being the one that keeps their word, even when it appears no one is looking.

6

Trust is an essential component of all relationships. And relationships are the power behind The Connector Effect™.

Before you'll generate referrals, Members of your Chapter have to know who you are, know what you do and know you are good at it. Quite simply, they must trust you. Only when you earn their trust will Members refer people to you.

The more Chapter meetings you attend, the more opportunities you'll have to foster stronger relationships with your fellow BNI Members.

The more Chapter meetings you attend, the more opportunities you'll have to foster stronger relationships with your fellow BNI Members.

While No One Can Take Your Place, a Substitute May Fill in for You When You Can't Attend

Substitutes often generate business when attending on behalf of BNI Members. Plus, it gives Chapter Members another person to refer to and build a relationship with. If you must miss a meeting, sending a suitable substitute is a great alternative.

Make a list of people who know how good you are at providing products or services:

- Other local businesspeople
- Clients and suppliers
- Your staff and sales representatives
- Industry colleagues
- Others you can call on with less notice
- Your spouse and family members
- Friends and other members
- Fellow team members in clubs/sports/volunteering you are involved with

Be strategic about who you line up to be your substitute at your BNI Chapter meeting. Consider lining up one of your best customers to attend as your substitute. That customer can give a great testimonial about you and the work you do. Your substitute is able to give your Chapter Members a more specific idea of your target customer without you even being at the meeting. The right guest can be a great referral generator for them and you.

Prepare your substitute for success:

1. Invite them to a meeting with you before the one you might miss so they feel comfortable with the format and know the location.

2. Connect them with a fellow Member to greet them and make introductions.

3. Prepare a Weekly Presentation for them to easily read at the meeting.

4. Give them a list of any referrals you have passed during the week so they can share this with the group.

5. Thank them for representing your business at the meeting.

The first month after James Yuille joined his BNI Chapter in Australia, he generated a referral that's still paying him today. That referral has generated more than $3 million in the 19 years since he joined. That referral changed his life and enabled him to transform his new, fledgling business into a growing enterprise.

The advice he gave the company that was referred to him has turned his small business into a multinational corporation. Today, he's generating more than $300,000 for his Google Ads consultancies each year.

"Make sure your BNI Chapter Members know who your ideal client is," James advises. "Consistent attendance and fitting your schedule around your BNI Chapter meeting is one of the keys to success."

"There is an uplifting spirit in a BNI Chapter. That spirit can't be transferred. Rather, it is generated by the Members and their personalities. It is highly motivating, and I love going to my Thursday morning BNI Chapter meeting to be enveloped with that spirit."

He goes on to say, "Business is about relationships. Without that trust, without that intimate knowledge of not just the Member's business but also about them as a person, it's difficult to pass high-level referrals."

As a Master Connector you are trusting Members of your Chapter to be there when you need them. You need them to deliver when you pass them a referral.

That's why you need to be there for them. You need to attend your Chapter meetings. Or in the rare instance you aren't able to attend, send a substitute who will make you look great.

Within your Chapter there are several systems that maximize the referrals you receive for the time you invest. We'll reveal these systems and how they work in Chapter 11.

But first, your Chapter includes additional opportunities to generate more referrals through leadership opportunities. We'll reveal how you can take advantage of those opportunities in the next chapter.

Chapter 10
Accelerating the Positive Impact to Your Business and Life

Dawn Kennedy felt like a stranger in her own hometown. She moved back to her old hometown after living in Florida for 20 years. The family business her uncle and father started in 1959 needed a flooring salesperson, so she rejoined the company.

Luckily, a family friend suggested she join a BNI Chapter at about the same time. Her sales the first year were $77,000, which helped her "hit the ground running."

Now in her second year, she began to serve within her BNI Chapter Leadership Team as Secretary/ Treasurer. In the first six months her closed sales totaled $84,000! This is all the more amazing because she had a bilateral hip replacement and was recovering for six weeks afterward. Members of her BNI Chapter continued to send her referrals. That enabled her to close $20,000 in written sales even while recovering from the operation.

The flooring business is traditionally cyclical, with the bulk of the sales coming during the summer months. However, Dawn has been able to maintain her gross sales even during the slow retail months because of her BNI referrals.

She has enjoyed becoming a Master Connector, helping her clients, friends and family increase their own chances of referrals. In conclusion, Dawn says about BNI, "The professionalism of the BNI Members has helped me raise my bar and become a better networker, speaker and all-around more confident and efficient sales professional."

You can accelerate your referrals and network growth by serving on your Chapter's Leadership Team. As a Chapter Leader you build trust by demonstrating your expertise. You also increase visibility as your Chapter gets to hear from you more often, and Chapter meetings are even more fun because you get to become a part of the action.

Your Chapter offers several leadership positions to distribute the time commitments. There are roles for many Members. Leadership opportunities give you great avenues for building your experience, networking and generating referrals.

Since 1985, BNI has been running Chapters efficiently by giving members well-defined leadership positions that help them generate more referrals and grow their network. As a Chapter Leader, you'll:

- Have more fun at meetings as you fulfill an important role in the meeting agenda;
- Learn valuable business lessons that'll make you a more effective leader of your own business;
- Make your Chapter more effective by stepping up into a role that has a big impact;
- Be eligible for bigger leadership opportunities within your BNI region, nationally and internationally, including attending BNI national conferences and maybe even BNI's Annual Global Convention; and
- Generate more referrals for your business as your leadership position enables you to build strong relationships even faster.

BNI Leadership Positions

Which leadership role is most interesting to you? Your Chapter has regular transitions so you can move from one position into others.

President

You get the most visibility in the Chapter by sharing your personality and leadership with the group. As President, you get to inspire both current Members and visitors alike to want to be a contributing Member of the Chapter by making the meeting the best part of everyone's week.

Vice President

In this role you get to turn your Chapter into a goal-achieving machine by helping set goals, inspiring Members to hop on board and helping Members stay accountable to the goals and dreams that each of them has. You also help ensure each Member is and continues to be a high-quality, developing businessperson. You do this through membership selection and through coaching each Member to be a better version of themselves.

Secretary/Treasurer

As Secretary/Treasurer you use your organizational skills to ensure the Chapter finances are in line and speakers are lined up. You can show your personality by introducing the featured presenter each week.

Education Coordinator

If you have lots of personality, awesome communication skills and a love for learning, being the Education

Coordinator provides you with the visibility to show your stuff.

Visitor Host

Do you love throwing dinner parties, introducing people to one another and making people feel hugely welcome? Join the Visitor Host Team and make each person feel like they are the most special person in the world.

Mentor Coordinator

Do you love coaching and mentoring? Do you have skills to share? The Mentor Coordinator helps make the new Member onboarding experience amazing. You get to make every new Member feel super special.

Membership Committee

The Membership Committee comprises two to four people to screen prospective Members to ensure they are a good fit for the Chapter. They also resolve any challenges within the Chapter. A great resource for Members of a Membership Committee who have implemented a mentoring program is *The Networking Mentor* co-authored by a co-author of this book and BNI Founder Ivan Misner, Ph.D.

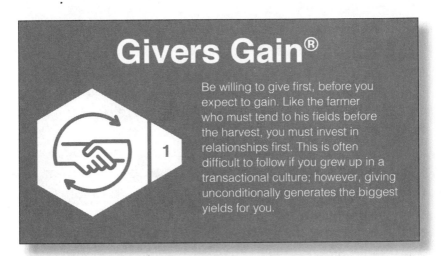

Givers Gain®

Be willing to give first, before you expect to gain. Like the farmer who must tend to his fields before the harvest, you must invest in relationships first. This is often difficult to follow if you grew up in a transactional culture; however, giving unconditionally generates the biggest yields for you.

Chapter Leadership is a remarkable example of the Givers Gain principle at work.

Many Members are already confident in their speaking, leadership and management skills. However, most discover that BNI Chapter Leadership enables them to develop their skills in a new way.

Leading a group of strong-willed businesspeople is different than the management experience you get within your own business. You'll be challenged. And it'll make you a better leader within your own business.

The best part is you'll be generating more referrals while you do it!

"I look for an area I think the Chapter could improve upon, and I volunteer for that position," says Phil Goodge, an insurance agent in the United States.

After being a BNI Member for 12 years, his residual policy premiums from BNI referrals are now greater than $250,000 per year. And the best referral he ever received was back in 2012 when a Chapter Member introduced him to an attractive lady who became his "BNI bride."

Phil has served within Chapter Leadership roles for 10 of the 12 years he's been a BNI Member. And he focuses on being very responsive when receiving a referral or any communication from a BNI Member, so much so that Members of his Chapter have given him the nickname "Get it done Goodge."

Phil is frequently thanked by clients when he refers them to fellow BNI Members. He has discovered that becoming a Master Connector who solves problems has increased his customer loyalty within his insurance agency. Plus, he's been able to get great professional advice he can share with his clients even when it doesn't involve a sale.

Phil does recommend patience and perseverance to anyone joining BNI. In year nine of his membership he received his largest referral so far. It's a client who spends $50,000 a year with his agency!

Phil does recommend patience and perseverance to anyone joining BNI. In year nine of his membership he received his largest referral so far. It's a client who spends $50,000 a year with his agency! Phil recommends, "If you make the effort to find referrals to give to other BNI Members, it comes back in many unexpected ways."

Chapter 11
Generate More Referrals in the Least Amount of Time

If you'd met the United Kingdom's Maggie Compton after she was kicked out of college because she didn't "toe the line," you'd never guess she would become a solicitor, start her own law firm and grow it in 10 years to have five locations and a staff of 40-plus serving clients around the world.

Her entry into the legal profession was a chance event. After she was asked to leave college, she used her shorthand skills to get a job at a solicitor's office. The manager spotted Maggie's potential and started her on the long journey to becoming a qualified solicitor herself. While she passed the exams with relative ease, becoming a solicitor was a long process. Maggie had to juggle responsibilities at school, work and home as she was a single mother for part of this time.

As a Master Connector, Maggie became known in her personal life as the "go-to person." Even though Maggie has been a BNI Member for 19 years, she says, "There is never a week that goes by that BNI hasn't generated something for me and my practice."

There's no more economical and efficient way to grow your business than becoming a Master Connector through your BNI Chapter. Within our Chapters around the world we've tested thousands of great ideas. Each Chapter tracks referrals passed, guests invited, Members retained and other items. It's easy to identify which ideas improve performance. We use those innovations to improve the system by replicating them around the world.

McDonald's is the largest franchise in the world, built on the strength of its business system. A French fry in Topeka, Kansas, tastes the same as a fry in New York City. And adjusting for regional preferences, it tastes the same as a fry in the United Kingdom.

McDonald's is always innovating. As a consumer we see they are testing new products all the time. They also test thousands of innovations within their business systems that we can't see. McDonald's measures sales revenues and profits before and after each innovation to decide which ideas should be rolled out to the rest of their locations.

We have a similar process at BNI. With Chapters around the world, we've discovered there are many new and developing regional best practices that can be incorporated into global systems and training.

Our rigorous testing is focused on creating as many new customers for Members' businesses as possible, and in the least amount of time.

Your BNI Chapter has a lot of systems. Each of these has been tested and then rolled out over the last several decades.

Tracking Referrals

What gets measured gets improved. The most effective way to lose weight is to track what you eat. You should track without judgment. You can use one of the many smart phone apps to make it more convenient. But when you see the number of calories and where they come from, you'll start making different choices.

It's the same with referrals for business passed within your Chapter. When you see your Chapter's goals for the business you want to generate, as each deadline approaches Members stretch themselves to reach the Chapter's goal.

Within BNI a tradition has formed to talk about the "seat value" of a given Chapter. This is just taking the total closed business divided by the number of Members. This is a fun measure to use to spur the healthy competitive spirit between BNI Chapters. It's designed to make it more fun to see which BNI Chapter can generate the most business by passing referrals.

This is a "game" that's, of course, very profitable for Members. The "score" represents customers served and money earned. What a great way to celebrate and achieve together!

While the seat value is a fun way to compare Chapters, it's important that you don't use it as a comparison to yourself. Every business is different. For some businesses it's easier to generate a lot of high-value referrals. Other business types cannot pass or receive that average value.

Some Members receive fewer referrals with a higher value. Other Chapter Members will receive a lot more referrals, but with lower values. That's perfectly alright.

Every seat brings value to the Chapter. And it's important that the Chapter brings value to every seat.

Tracking is about making the business of passing referrals more fun. And it's been proven to increase the performance of the Chapter for every Member.

Weekly Meetings

"BNI is great; if only the meetings were every other week," or "Why don't Chapters meet monthly? Weekly is too often," are the most frequent suggestions we hear. And that's worldwide.

Over the last several decades, there have been Chapters full of smart, ambitious Members who have tried meeting biweekly or monthly. Each time referrals plummet by as much as 52%!

Your BNI Chapter meets each week because research proves Weekly Meetings generate the most referrals for your business. Weekly Meetings enable you to build relationships and your Chapter to develop a better understanding of your business and the types of people to refer to you. Frequent, consistent communication is a proven model for building trust and generating more referrals.

Every one of the hundreds of thousands of BNI Members around the world are busy businesspeople, just like you are. They'd love to meet less often, if we could. But what we've discovered is Weekly Meetings are what it takes to build a strong referral network.

Weekly Meetings are one of the important elements of your shortcut to becoming a Master Connector.

Agenda

Wasting time in unproductive meetings has become a cliché in business. To avoid wasting your time, since 1985 every BNI Chapter meeting is run by an agenda. Each item on the agenda represents an innovation that generates more referrals for Members.

Here's a quick summary of the key parts of the meeting agenda to accelerate your success:

Open Networking – The meeting begins punctually with 15 minutes of open time for Members to build stronger relationships with each other and to meet visitors. Use this time to foster stronger relationships with Members you know and initiate relationships with Members you haven't connected with. Plus, make a point to meet visitors and welcome them to your Chapter.

Welcome – The President welcomes everyone to the Chapter meeting and invites them to take their seats. The President then welcomes visitors and introduces the Chapter Leadership.

Purpose & Overview of BNI – The President recognizes a Member to share the impact BNI has had on their business. Consider if there's someone you know who would appreciate hearing this story to encourage them to visit your BNI Chapter.

Networking Education – The Education Coordinator (or a Member assigned in advance by the Education Coordinator) delivers a 3-5 minute presentation on networking. Always look for opportunities to improve one of the most important skills of Master Connectors.

Announce BNI Network Leaders – During the first meeting of the month, the President recognizes Members who made remarkable efforts in the previous month. Make a note to congratulate

Members on their achievements to become Master Connectors themselves. And study what successful Members do that make them so effective. Then, with a fun competitive spirit, make plans to go beat them next month.

Pass Business Card Box – Within 23 minutes into meeting, the President begins to pass around the business card box. This box includes business cards of each Member. Ensure you have a business card from each Member of your BNI Chapter referral network to make it easier for you to pass referrals during the week.

Welcome New/Renewing Members to the Organization – Within 24 minutes into the meeting, new and renewing Members are invited to the front of the room for recognition by the Chapter. Make a note to recognize these important milestones with a text, email or phone call to these Members.

Members Introduce Themselves & Give their Weekly Presentations – Each Member has the opportunity to introduce themselves, explain to Members what they do and ask for connections to their best target customers. While listening to each Member, consider whether over the last week you've heard anyone using the language of referrals to signal the opportunity for referrals.

Vice President's Report – To keep Members excited about generating referrals, the Vice President gives the "PALMS Report" providing the average number of monthly referrals, average number of monthly visitors and the total referrals to date. Identify where you are on the report and consider how you can pass more referrals and sponsor more Members to practice Givers Gain® and increase the results of your Chapter.

Membership Committee Report – This report updates Members on the professions needed by the Chapter as well as the status of pending membership applications. Fill in gaps within your referral network by inviting visitors and sponsoring new Members.

Secretary/Treasurer Announces Speaker Rotation – The Secretary/Treasurer announces the speakers for the next six weeks and introduces this meeting's speaker using the Member's biography sheet. Pass along any questions you have to upcoming featured speakers. It will help each Member give a better presentation by customizing it for the needs of fellow Members.

Speaker(s) Give 5-12 Minute Feature Presentation(s), Including Questions & Answers – One or two Members provide a presentation that gives Members greater clarity as to the target market and business to help generate more referrals. Always listen with a "beginner's mind." Look for new ideas or for things you used to know, but may have recently forgotten.

Referrals & Testimonials – All Members stand for this, the most important part of the meeting. Members report referrals given or provide a testimonial for any Member of the Chapter. Make the decision to set aside the time throughout the week to ensure you always have a referral to report or a testimonial to provide.

Referral Reality Check – The Vice President chooses two referral slips from two weeks prior and asks the Members who shared them to stand to report the outcome to the Chapter. Consider what makes a quality referral so you can strive to become the best Master Connector you can be.

Secretary/Treasurer Report – This report alerts Members if they are up for renewal. Make a note so you can tell any renewing Members that you look forward to their contributions each week and hope they will choose to remain part of your referral network.

President Thanks Visitors – The President excuses visitors to another room to speak with the Visitor Host for more information to consider applying for membership in the Chapter.

BNI Announcements, Reminders & Special Reports – These include any announcements about networking events, Member training programs or other regional activities. Make sure all the important dates are on your calendar.

Door Prize Drawing(s), for Members Bringing Visitors or Referrals – The Vice President conducts a drawing for any Members passing referrals or bringing visitors to the meeting.

Close Meeting – Within 90 minutes (or longer for larger Chapters) of the beginning of the Open Networking portion of the meeting, the President closes with a positive quote and encourages Members to bring referrals and/or visitors to the next meeting. Make an appointment on your calendar with yourself to ensure you handle the quick follow-up items you noted throughout the meeting. Examples include passing referrals, recognizing Members and scheduling One-to-Ones.

It's the same agenda every week to make it simple to learn and follow. And there's a script to run the meeting to increase the number of referrals passed to Members. An agenda with a script focuses attention on the Members, and the repetition leads to every Member solidly knowing every other Member's business.

While we often test different agendas and scripts, our focus is on helping you connect with your Chapter. This is to give you visibility within the Chapter. And most of all, it's meant to create an environment that generates as many referrals for your business as possible.

Referrals & Testimonials

Your BNI Chapter meeting includes two items you'll want to prepare for.

First, you have your Weekly Presentation. You learned how to prepare for this in Chapter 5. When you follow the BNI system, you'll learn how to improve and align all of the marketing materials you produce. Plus, this structure will help you become more comfortable with public speaking even if the thought strikes fear in you today.

The second section to prepare for is called Referrals & Testimonials.

Each week, every member is expected to contribute something important during the Referrals & Testimonials portion of the meeting.

It's always easy to do one of the following two things:

- I have a referral for ...
- I have a written testimonial for ...

BNI Chapters don't let Members pass during this portion of the agenda. You'll find that if you let a Member pass once, then they'll take a pass at future meetings. It's important that every Member of your BNI Chapter contributes each week.

While making your time at the Chapter meeting as effective as possible, you'll want to invest time into your Chapter and yourself between Chapter meetings as well.

Member Success Program

To accelerate your success, BNI provides the BNI Member Success Program (MSP). MSP is a video training program that trains on the important skills Members need to become successful Master Connectors within BNI.

Members who complete MSP receive more referrals.

We've discovered that Members who complete MSP receive more referrals. They get better results. Thus, we've created a further incentive to encourage new Members to complete MSP as quickly as possible after joining BNI.

Within each Chapter meeting agenda is a 10-minute slot for a Feature Presentation. This presentation is provided by a Member. These Feature Presentations are educational for Members. Plus, they give Members a more specific mental picture of who they should refer to the presenter.

We briefly referred to Feature Presentations in the Melissa Overton story in Chapter 1. And then we told you about how George Johnson gave a presentation on the challenges of dealing with aging parents. These are examples of the great opportunities you have in BNI to share your experience and to develop your public speaking skills.

Many Members experience a surge in referrals after giving a Feature Presentation. After all, Members become more familiar with your range of expertise. This sparks more connections for you.

After you complete MSP, you'll be added to the roster of eligible Members to give a Feature Presentation for your Chapter. This gives Members an incentive to get MSP completed. And it ensures their presentations are informational for the Chapter because they've been trained on what BNI is all about.

After MSP, new Members are more prepared to give a great Feature Presentation that's informative for Members and generates more referrals.

BNI Policies – Rules of the Game

To ensure your BNI Chapter is an effective investment of your time, BNI's International Board of Advisors, consisting of BNI Members from around the world, creates and reviews these policies on an ongoing basis.

This one-pager is the foundation of the BNI system. It's intended to protect you. It's designed to ensure you are able to generate as much business as possible from BNI, and in the least possible time. BNI's Member Policies and Code of Ethics are included in the Appendix of this book.

BNI Connect® Mobile

BNI provides a smart phone app that allows you to conduct most of your BNI business with just a few taps. All Google Android users can get the app for free from the Google Play Store. Apple iPhone users can download the BNI Connect app from the App Store.

Here's a quick listing of what you'll discover on the BNI Connect Mobile app:

Member Profile – You can update your Member profile to make it easy for your Chapter Members to pass you referrals. This is also an effective way to connect with hundreds of thousands BNI Members from other Chapters around the world.

Referral Slips – Chapter 7 explains how to give referrals. This is where you record them. Complete this form and report your referral at your next Chapter meeting.

Thank You for Closed Business – The Thank You for Closed Business program is how your Chapter tracks the value of referrals given using the BNI system. When we say we've passed 11.2 million in referrals it's because this is tracked closely within BNI. Posting Thank You for Closed Business is a great way to demonstrate your appreciation for BNI Members who pass referrals to you. When someone receives a Thank You for Closed Business, they are going to feel good about being recognized for practicing Givers Gain by passing referrals.

Complete this form with the name of the Member who gave you the referral and the value of the referral (gross revenue). The person whose name you enter on the Thank You for Closed Business will get credit for generating business in the dollar amount you list. Your name, as the person who received the dollar amount, remains anonymous.

Chapter Education Unit Slips – BNI provides a wide range of training for Members to grow professionally while learning the tools to grow their business. After each training, submit a CEU slip to indicate which training or workshop you attended. There are promotions and incentives for the Chapter generating the most CEUs per Member.

One-to-One Follow-up Slips – After each One-to-One, the Member who initiated the One-to-One completes this slip. This enables your Chapter to compete in periodic promotions to incentivize One-to-One meetings.

Written Testimonials – Use this form when you do business with a fellow Member and the experience is so good that you're ready to give a written testimonial.

You'll want to take the opportunity to update your Member Profile as quickly as possible. It's an opportunity for you to promote your business to hundreds of thousands of people throughout the world.

We often hear stories of BNI Members contacted by someone across the country or even overseas who is looking for someone they can trust to support a friend or loved one. Today, a lot of BNI Members use the BNI Connect Mobile app when they travel to look for business opportunities while visiting other countries for vacation.

We cannot guarantee that if you have a complete profile that you'll get a referral from the BNI Connect Mobile app. However, if you don't complete your profile we can guarantee you won't get referrals through the BNI Connect Mobile app. It is quick and easy, so it makes sense to do it right away.

Gold Club Recognition

You'll discover BNI has a lot of ways to recognize Members and incentivize success, just like you should for your team within your own business.

Earning a Gold Club recognition is a prestigious achievement for BNI Members. You earn your Gold Club recognition when you sponsor six or more Members into BNI. Some Chapters use badges while others present pins to Members achieving Gold Club status.

Local Trainings

There are BNI meetings within your community, region and nation, as well the international community. Plus there are BNI Connect Webinars, local training events and podcasts you can learn from.

Ask your Chapter Leaders for your regional events calendar to take advantage of these opportunities.

BNI U

As your business grows you'll encounter new challenges. Problems arise in a $5 million-a-year business that don't exist in a $1 million-a-year company. Recruiting employees, creating business systems, sales training, leadership and everything else can become overwhelming for businesspeople to master.

BNI U is your one-stop source for information on scaling your growing company. BNI Members around the world have encountered similar challenges. You can learn from their experiences and from the best subject matter experts to accelerate your business growth.

You'll learn more about the resources available within BNI U as you engage with your BNI Chapter. For now, know that we understand what businesspeople go through and we want to do everything possible to make it easier to grow your business.

BNI Online

During 2020, in-person meetings became impossible.

BNI prioritized safety above all other considerations. When this situation first arose, BNI Leaders around the world deployed BNI Online.

This platform enabled BNI Chapters to transition to online meetings on a temporary basis so they can continue supporting each other and passing referrals in any situation.

BNI is emerging from this situation stronger than ever. Some Chapters will continue meeting via BNI Online while the rest of the world transitions back to in-person meetings.

Antonio Lopez, one of the owners of Ortegal Oil, a network of automobile service stations in Spain, has been a BNI Member since 2016. BNI Online has enabled Antonio to form business relationships around the world, converting 10 referrals into closed business.

Speaking of his experience with BNI Online, Antonio says, "If there is one thing I learned during this time, it is that BNI Online is a fundamental tool. Just because your business is closed and you are confined to home doesn't mean you are stopped. BNI Online has enabled me to continue growing my business while my competition has been inactive."

Traditions + Innovation

Traditions tell us who we are. Innovation tells us where we want to go. You need to know who you are as an organization, and you need to know where you are going as an organization. This keeps you from losing your place in the world while you continue to strive to create a better life for yourself and others.

4

Although BNI has changed in a thousand ways in the last several decades, the foundation remains the same as when the organization was started in 1985.

Once upon a time, BNI Members had to hand write referral slips. Passing a referral meant literally handing a fellow Member a slip of paper. Today all that's been replaced with the BNI Connect Mobile app. The app has made it a lot easier to be a BNI Member by having all the forms, tracking and Member data in one place. And yet, the key elements of referrals, agendas and relationships have remained the same.

This is the essence of the BNI Core Value Traditions + Innovation. You always retain your core values even while you strive to improve yourself. This keeps you from falling for the latest passing fad while you strive to get better.

Aurore Delsoir made a big change in her professional life. She left behind 14 years in the pharmaceutical industry to pursue her passion for photography in Belgium.

"People told me, 'You're absolutely mad! You're not going to leave a good, stable income just like that?'" To her critics, Aurore answered, "I'm not crazy. But yes, I'm going to make a change."

And just like that, Aurore became a self-employed photographer. It was difficult in the beginning. But she didn't give up. She discovered BNI and joined her local Chapter.

"The BNI method really spoke to me. The structure, the Givers Gain Core Value. And it's true that everyone was very nice, too."

Aurore dove into her BNI Chapter, taking portraits of each of her fellow Members. She invited 15 guests per month to her Chapter. And she became a Master Connector referring fellow Members whenever she could. This generated more and more referrals for Aurore. In less than a year her photography business went from a part-time venture to her full-time vocation.

Whether you have been in business for many decades or you're creating a business for the first time, the BNI system is here to help you reach your business and life goals.

Whether you have been in business for many decades or you're creating a business for the first time, the BNI system is here to help you reach your business and life goals.

Chapter 12

A Week in the Life of a Master Connector
(Ok, it's a week and two days) ☺

As an optometrist in the Philippines, John Paul Lam did what most optometrists do to get new clients: He relied on walk-ins and client referrals. However, he discovered this was slow.

After his friend invited him to attend a local BNI Chapter meeting, he joined because the Members were so professional and sincere.

As a result of joining, he has increased his sales by 20%. He's extremely happy about how BNI changed his business. He's now reaching monthly sales figures that broke the record for the highest sales in years.

But his favorite part of BNI is being able to help others as a Master Connector. As John says, "No 'ifs,' 'ands' or 'buts,' but helping with all my heart."

You've had the opportunity to learn all the pieces of becoming a Master Connector. Don't expect to be perfect in your first few months. Just as if you were learning to play tennis, hit a golf ball, or learn how to swim, you'll improve with practice.

As a Master Connector you can become good in a few weeks. And in a few months of practice you will be great.

To help you form a mental picture of what life is like as a Master Connector, here's a week in the life of a fictional Member named Mary.

Mary has been a Member for six months now, and her Chapter's help has changed the way she gives and gets business. Her Chapter meets on Tuesdays.

This is how she has integrated BNI into her everyday life:

Monday:

Mary starts by opening up the BNI Connect® Mobile app and recording a referral (Thank You for Closed Business) she received last week that converted into a nice sale. She has made a mental note to say "thank you" to the Member who passed her that referral during the Open Networking portion of her Chapter meeting.

Mary then creates her Weekly Presentation to get ready for the next day's meeting.

Tuesday:

Mary attends the BNI meeting and makes a successful presentation that is well received by her Chapter. Afterward, she wants to meet up with John. She hasn't had the opportunity to build a relationship with him in the last six months. John is within her contact sphere, meaning their businesses share a lot of the same customers. There are a lot of opportunities to pass referrals to each other.

Mary and her fellow Members stay back, trying to connect and discuss the referrals requested during the Weekly Presentations. They also discuss the status of referrals that have already been made, and they make calls to try to close those opportunities for each other.

Mary asks John for a One-to-One. They set their meeting for Thursday during lunch at a fellow Member's local restaurant.

She returns to her office for her weekly staff meeting, which she moved to Tuesdays following her BNI Chapter meeting.

At the start of the meeting, Mary shares the names of BNI Members who asked for introductions. If anyone on the team is able to help, Mary will work with that person to make the introductions for her fellow Members.

She pins the remaining list of requested introductions to the staff board just as a reminder. Everyone in her business now recognizes how important BNI is to them, as it's providing new business every month.

Wednesday:

On her way home from work, Mary visits the grocery store to pick up what she needs for dinner. As she pulls a credit card out of her wallet to pay, the cashier rubs his neck and complains he hasn't been able to sleep at night because of the pain he's feeling.

Mary asks if he would like to know the name of a good chiropractor. She explains that she has used them for treatment and they have really helped her. He says yes, so she gives him the chiropractor's card and says if he wants, she can use the BNI Connect Mobile app to get the office to call him and let him know when he can come in.

Mary gets the cashier's phone number, and she gets excited. It's only been one day and she already has a referral to present during the Referral portion of next week's Chapter meeting.

After dinner she completes a referral slip for the chiropractor within the BNI Connect Mobile app. This way, the cashier can expect a call from the chiropractor's office the next morning.

Thursday:

Meeting John for lunch is Mary's top priority for the day because they both have the same contact sphere. She knows they share a lot of potential clients but haven't built up a strong enough understanding of each other's business to be able to provide referrals.

They have a great One-to-One over lunch. As it turns out, they each have clients they can refer to each other. While at lunch they each make a call for the other to give them an introduction and pass a referral.

That evening, Mary records the referral slip and the One-to-One within BNI Connect. Now she has two referrals to give during that portion of the next meeting. She's already in the running for top referrals, and this will keep her there.

Friday:

Mary meets with the referral she received from John in Thursday's One-to-One. Since joining BNI, sales have become a lot easier. Because she was introduced through a referral from someone they trust, customers are happy to work with her to solve their problems. This proves true again as she's able to close the business. Mary turns the referral over to her team to complete the job.

Mary opens up the BNI Connect Mobile app on her phone to record a Thank You for Closed Business. She also pulls out her stationery, an envelope and a pen to write a thank-you note to John. Sure, it's part of BNI to pass referrals. But Mary is a Master Connector. Everyone gets a thank-you note.

Mary makes a call to Alex. He's a friend she went to school with. Her Chapter is looking for a good interior designer to join their network. The Chapter's architect is looking to refer work to one, and he'd be a good fit.

Alex is interested. Even though he's a great interior designer, he knows he has a lot to learn when it comes to getting new clients. After the call, Mary sends Alex an invite through the BNI Connect Mobile app. This will ensure Alex has all the meeting details, and it allows Mary to put Alex's name on the visitor list for the next meeting.

Saturday:

In BNI U, Mary listens to the BNI Official Podcast by Ivan Misner, Ph.D. It's a great way for her to continue her lifelong learning while completing errands for the week.

Sunday:

While Mary is visiting with her parents, her father asks Mary for a referral to a landscaper. Mary's father knows all about BNI and the Members involved.

Evidently, her dad's neighbor wants some work done in her backyard. Mary gives her father the number and asks for the neighbor's contact details to pass on to the landscape architect. Her dad calls the neighbor and lets her know the landscaper will be giving her a call.

Mary enters the neighbor's contact information into a referral slip in the BNI Connect Mobile app. Now she has three referrals to present at the next meeting.

Monday:

Mary calls Alex to remind him to come to the meeting. She tells Alex she'll personally introduce him to the architect. Alex confirms that he'll be there.

Mary also prepares her Weekly Presentation making sure she has a specific request—a company name and person she wishes to be connected to this week.

Tuesday:

Mary arrives early to the meeting to make sure she's there to greet Alex when he arrives.

She's satisfied with herself because she received a referral that she was able to close; she also completed a One-to-One, invited a visitor to the Chapter and passed three referrals during the week. She's excited to see where she stands in her BNI Chapter's Top Producer contest this month.

What do you think? Could you become a Master Connector to grow your business? It's as easy as that.

It's always a challenge to summarize the experience of hundreds of thousands of businesspeople in dozens of countries around the world. Your experience will be different because your business is different; you are in a unique city, and your BNI Chapter is full of unique people.

Give yourself time. If this is your first exposure to BNI, don't be intimidated if any of Mary's experiences appear to be difficult or foreign. Mary has been a Member for just under a year and has gone through the new member onboarding (BNI Member Success Program) to help her learn all these skills. She's going to be more familiar with BNI's strategies, and things will come easier for her than for someone who's just beginning.

Even as a beginner, you can be effective in BNI. The most important step on any journey is the next one.

However, even as a beginner, you can be effective in BNI. The most important step on any journey is the next one. And it's almost time to take your next step toward becoming a Master Connector.

Joanne Tang is a commercial interior designer from Hong Kong. She was no good at getting clients to refer her to their friends and family so she could expand her base of customers.

Today, she's grown her business by more than 40% since she joined her BNI Chapter. Becoming a Master Connector has enabled her to work more closely with her new referral partners, the Members of her BNI Chapter.

Chapter 13

An Easier Way to Grow a Business That Fulfills Your Dreams

The owner of an office janitorial firm in the Philippines, Djarna Pestano used to rely on "word of mouth referrals" to generate new clients. Since joining BNI she has generated more than $63 million in new clients in just over a year.

Yes, that's right. A member of her BNI Chapter was friends with the decision maker of a large telephone service provider. They needed a team of 169 janitors starting within two days! Djarna stepped up and made it happen. Thanks to that referral, she has an annual agreement.

BNI didn't start off easy for Djarna. Traffic is terrible in the Philippines. To attend her first BNI meeting at 6:45 am, she had to wake up at 4:30 am and leave by 6:00 am. She had her doubts as to whether these early morning commutes would be worth it.

In addition to the early mornings, the annual membership fee initially looked like a lot of money. That's when a Member seated beside her suggested she just divide that amount by 12. He told her that's a lot cheaper than trying to hire a marketing staff to generate the same amount of business.

That and the philosophy of Givers Gain® helped Djarna make the decision to join her BNI Chapter. Djarna observed that businesspeople are like crabs in a bucket, fighting against each other to get ahead. Within a BNI Chapter you are in a category of one without direct competitors. You are in a room full of Givers trying to help you grow.

"BNI made me alive again," says Djarna. "My life seemed to be on a plateau before I joined BNI." Djarna attributes a lot of her success to One-to-One meetings. She makes a point of using the products and services of her BNI Chapter Members. From water purifiers to outsourcing her company's payroll services, she has experienced a lot of benefits from BNI beyond business growth.

Establishing yourself as a Master Connector within your community is the key to growing your business.

Your BNI Chapter gives you a network you can trust to refer your friends, family and best customers. It's a group of businesspeople you trust to do what they promise. And because they trust you to do the same, they pass referrals of their friends, family and customers to you.

Your BNI Chapter gives you a network you can trust to refer your friends, family and best customers. It's a group of businesspeople you trust to do what they promise. And because they trust you to do the same, they pass referrals of their friends, family and customers to you.

BNI is different from every new customer acquisition system because of its accountability. You'll be able to monitor your return on investment every step of the way.

Becoming a Master Connector changes how you're perceived by your customers, friends and family. You become the hero they call when they have a problem. And you have a network of experts within the BNI Connect® Mobile app to solve problems that arise.

BNI has been around for several decades. And because hundreds of thousands of businesspeople in dozens of countries around the world use the BNI system to grow their businesses, you know it will be around for decades more.

At the same time, today's systems are new. There is a new world of opportunities to access by connecting to BNI Members across the globe.

You've had the opportunity to "meet" more than 20 BNI Members from around the world within the pages of this book. They volunteered their stories because they are so passionate about the impact BNI has had on their business. And they are passionate about the impact BNI can have on you and your business.

Within your local BNI Chapter there's plenty of proof that BNI works and works well. It's right there in flesh and blood. It's proof that BNI works within your own community.

You may have tried networking or passing referrals in the past. Most of us have. Outside of BNI there are so many reasons networking doesn't work. For most of us, one referral that goes wrong is reason enough to never try it again.

Businesspeople outside of BNI don't have the same motivation to protect their referral sources. As a Master Connector, your fellow Members want to keep receiving your referrals. Thus, if something does go wrong, they have a strong incentive to make it right. They want to do a good job for the customer because they are accountable to you through your BNI Chapter.

Every business group trying to fill events touts "great networking" as a reason to attend. "Networking" has become a generic term for standing around a cocktail party, hoping a person will show up that you already know so you have someone to talk to. These promoters have "watered" down the idea of networking. As you've seen within this book, BNI is completely different.

Networking as a Master Connector is about solving problems. And your BNI Chapter gives you the opportunity to network in a competitor-free environment. There's no more having to go to a networking event and ending up at the same table with two of your competitors.

How long do you want to continue missing out on so many referrals trying to run your business by yourself? How many months can you tolerate spending money on marketing that's not generating results? BNI Chapters in your area can only accept one business from your category. It's important that you secure your spot now and become a Master Connector.

All BNI Members around the world are businesspeople, just like you. We understand what it's like to go to unstructured and unproductive networking events. And we understand what it's like to come home with a stack of business cards but no new relationships. We know what it's like to spend money on advertising and see no return. We know what it's like to be out there alone, trying to figure out how to make it in business today. And we've discovered a better way. We invite you to give it a try.

You've already discovered how the BNI system works within this book. You'll receive more details through the BNI Member Success Program and from Members of your Chapter.

You may already be a BNI Member or on the path to becoming a Member. We'll outline the steps so you will know the best way to continue your membership journey.

Here is how you become a member:

1. Visit a BNI Chapter as a visitor. Consider visiting a few Chapters to find the one that feels like the best fit for you.

2. Complete the membership application and submit it with your payment.

3. After the Membership Committee reviews your application, you are notified when your Membership has been approved.

4. Complete the BNI Member Success Program.

5. Block out the time and dates for your Chapter meetings (Chapter 9).

6. Plan your first Weekly Presentation (Chapter 5).

7. Set a goal of completing one effective One-to-One each week (Chapter 6).

8. Become a Master Connector, listening for opportunities to pass referrals to your fellow Members (Chapter 7).

9. Make a list of visitors to invite to a Chapter meeting (Chapter 8).

In the United States, 50% of businesses fail within the first five years. And this failure rate is higher around the world. While we cannot guarantee that your business will succeed and grow when you become a Master Connector, it will certainly be a lot harder to succeed if you don't join BNI.

You've seen more than 20 examples of businesspeople around the world who have used BNI to grow their business beyond their expectations. They did all this by becoming a Master Connector.

You've seen the entire system. It's simple. It's easy to implement. And it's remarkably effective.

Now it's time for a decision: Will you become a Master Connector and put The Connector Effect™ to work in your business and your life?

At this point you have three options:

Option #1: Do absolutely nothing and stay exactly where you are right now.

Do this if you already have enough money to retire and you're not worried about having new customer referrals to grow your business.

If that's the case, maybe you don't need to use the Master Connector strategy.

Option #2: Do it yourself.

You can try to build a network of professionals to whom you can refer. You can attempt to train and motivate them on how to pass referrals to you.

If you are willing to work hard and spend hours reinventing an entire referral system from scratch, you might be able to pull it off.

Option #3: Let your BNI Chapter do the heavy lifting for you.

You'll put the proven BNI system to work for your business. You'll engage the businesspeople within your BNI Chapter that are standing ready to learn more about you and your business goals so they can pass referrals to you.

Half of all businesses close within five years of getting started. You've got a much better chance of success with BNI than you do without it.

You'll get to enjoy running your business. You'll be able to focus more time doing what you do best. This is because you've got a team dedicated to helping you find customers.

And your customers, friends and family will begin to turn to you because you've become a Master Connector. You'll build more trust with your customers. You'll be able to walk into a room full of strangers and solve problems for anyone who is lucky enough to meet you.

Your BNI Chapter as well as hundreds of thousands of BNI Members around the world stand ready to help you grow your business. That is, if you'll let us help you. You must take the first steps.

Are you ready to put the power of The Connector Effect into your business and your life? Will you become a Master Connector?

Only you can decide.

For Further Study

Here is a list of resources for Master Connectors who want to accelerate their success in business and within their life.

BNI Training Resources

Because Lifelong Learning is a Core Value of BNI's Membership, we make a lot of training resources available to you.

BNI's Member Success Program

An online program, it helps you learn each of the skills you need to be a successful Member of BNI. Once you become a Member you will receive access to BNI U and be assigned each class you need when you need it.

BNI Key Skills Workshops

Programs are offered regularly in your local area where you can go practice all the things you have learned in the Member Success Program. You can find more information in the event section of your regional BNI site.

BNI Advanced Skills Workshops

These classes help you further advance your communications, presentation and referral skills so you can continue your quest to becoming a Master Connector. You can find more information in the event section of your regional BNI site.

BNI National Conferences

These conferences are opportunities to come learn from Master Connectors in your country. To find more information, go to the BNI Country website.

BNI Annual Global Convention
BNIGlobalEvents.com

This Convention builds relationships with thousands of businesspeople from around the world. While there are several educational programs, the event is about making connections, building existing relationships and celebrating what Members around the world have achieved together.

Networking

Books by the Founder, Ivan Misner, Ph.D.:

The World's Best Known Marketing Secret (4th Edition)
Networking Like a Pro (2nd Edition)
The 29% Solution, 52 Weekly Networking Success Strategies
The Networking Mentor
Room Full of Referrals

Books by Other Networking Experts:

Endless Referrals by Bob Burg
The Go Giver by Bob Burg
How to Work a Room by Susan RoAne
The Little Black Book of Connections by Jeffrey Gitomer
Dig Your Well Before You're Thirsty by Harvey Mackay

Business Books

The Retention Point by Robert Skrob
Success Principles by Jack Canfield
The 21 Irrefutable Laws of Leadership by John Maxwell
Love is Damn Good Business by Steve Farber
Masters of Success by Dr. Ivan Misner
The E-Myth by Michael Gerber
The Little Red Book of Selling by Jeffrey Gitomoer
Good to Great by Jim Collins
Conscious Capitalism by Mackey and Sisodia
Inside the Magic Kingdom by Tom Connellan
The Speed of Trust by Stephen M. R. Covey
Pop! by Sam Horn
*The 100 Absolutely Unbreakable Laws of Business
Success* by Brian Tracy
Guerilla Marketing by Jay Conrad Levinson

Personal Development Books

Who's in Your Room by Dr. Ivan Misner
Chicken Soup for the Soul by Canfield and Hansen
Think and Grow Rich by Napoleon Hill
The Passion Test by Attwood and Attwood
How to Stop Worrying and Start Living by Dale Carnegie
How I Raised Myself from Failure to Success in Selling
   by Frank Bettger

BNI Diversity Statement and Policies

BNI's Core Values Start with Givers Gain®

The altruism and goodwill we feel towards one another, and to the world, start with a genuine love of people—all people, equally. We encourage and embrace diversity in every respect.

Our Statement on Equality and Non-discrimination

BNI requires that Chapters review and select persons for membership in all job classifications based on qualifications without regard to race, color, gender, religion, national origin, marital status, sexual orientation, age or disability. BNI will support no Chapter's action when in violation of this equality and non-discrimination statement.

BNI's General Policies

Membership Committees of each chapter have final authority related to BNI® Policies. Membership Committees may put a Member on probation or open a Member's classification for failure to comply with the Member Policies, the Code of Ethics or BNI® Core Values.

1. Only one person from each BNI classification can join a chapter of BNI®. Each Member can only hold one BNI classification in a BNI Chapter.

2. Members should represent their primary professional focus.

3. Members must arrive on time and stay for the entire published meeting time.

4. An individual can only be a Member of one BNI® Chapter. A Member cannot be in any other program that holds Members accountable for passing referrals.

5. A Member is allowed three absences within a continuous six-month period. If a Member cannot attend, they may send a substitute; this will not count as an absence.

6. Members are expected to be engaged in the BNI Chapter by bringing qualified referrals and/or visitors.

7. Visitors may attend chapter meetings up to two times.

8. Only BNI Members, BNI Directors/Director Consultants can do Feature Presentations during the BNI Meetings.

9. There are no leaves of absence except for medical leaves.

10. Members who wish to change their BNI classification must submit a new membership application for approval.

11. All BNI membership lists are for the purpose of giving referrals only. Before sending any other

communication to BNI Members or Director/
Director Consultants, the person must give their
consent. Consent must be freely given, specific,
informed and unambiguous.

12. All new Members must complete the Member
Success Program.

Note: All BNI policies are subject to change. All proposed
policy changes need to be reviewed first by BNI's
International Board of Advisors.

The Core Values of the Successful Master Connector

Givers Gain®

Be willing to give first, before you expect to gain. Like the farmer who must tend to his fields before the harvest, you must invest in relationships first. This is often difficult to follow if you grew up in a transactional culture; however, giving unconditionally generates the biggest yields for you.

Building Relationships

No one is successful on their own. Becoming good at developing relationships, creating a network of support and always growing your network are the keys to success in business and in life.

Lifelong Learning

Your value grows as you develop your knowledge and skills. Our world is in a constant state of change. Unless you are learning, you are falling behind. Create a curriculum based on the person you want to become, and follow that curriculum to get yourself there.

Traditions + Innovation

Traditions tell us who we are. Innovation tells us where we want to go. You need to know who you are as an organization, and you need to know where you are going as an organization.This keeps you from losing your place in the world while you continue to strive to create a better life for yourself and others.

Positive Attitude

The habit of finding the good in everything that happens to you propels your life beyond setbacks. Those who see the best in situations, others and themselves magnetically attract people, opportunities and wealth.

Accountability

The fastest way to build trust is to make promises and keep them. Rather than expecting others to believe you and accept your word, demonstrate who you are by accepting leadership roles, following through on your promises and being the one that keeps their word, even when it appears no one is looking.

Recognition

Tell the people around you that you appreciate what they've accomplished for themselves, you and the organization. Recognition is the fuel that builds organizations and societies. The person who masters the art of recognition attracts a strong network and leads a fulfilling life.

The Connector Effect™

GAINS Exchange Profile

Goals	Goals	
Goals are the business or personal objectives you want or need to meet for yourself or the people who are important to you. You need to define your goals and have a clear picture of the other person's goals. The best way to build a relationship with someone is to help them achieve their goals.		
Accomplishments	**Accomplishments**	
People like to talk about the things they are proud of. Remember, some of your best insight into others comes from knowing what goals they have already achieved. Your knowledge, skills, experiences and value can be surmised from your achievements. Be ready to share your accomplishments with the people you meet.		
Interests	**Interests**	
Your interests can help you connect with others. Interests are things like playing sports, reading books and listening to music. People like to spend time with those who share their interests.		
Networks	**Networks**	
You have many networks, both formal and informal. A network can be an organization, institution, company or individual you associate with.		
Skills	**Skills**	
The more you know about the talents and abilities of the people in your network the better equipped you are to find (and refer!) competent affordable products and services when the need arises.		

About the Authors

Ivan Misner, Ph.D.

Dr. Misner's Ph.D. is from the University of Southern California. He is a *New York Times* best-selling author who has written 24 books including one of his latest books—*Who's in Your Room?* He is also a columnist for Entrepreneur.com and has been a university professor as well as a member of the Board of Trustees for the University of La Verne.

Called the "Father of Modern Networking" by both Forbes and CNN, Dr. Misner is considered to be one of the world's leading experts on business networking and has been a keynote speaker for major corporations and associations throughout the world. He has been featured in the *L.A. Times*, *The Wall Street Journal* and *The New York Times*, as well as numerous TV and radio shows including CNN, the BBC and the *Today Show* on NBC.

Among his many awards, he has been named "Humanitarian of the Year" by the Red Cross and was recently the recipient of the John C. Maxwell Leadership Award. He is also proud to be the Co-Founder of the BNI Charitable Foundation. He and his wife, Elisabeth, are now "empty nesters" with three adult children Oh, and in his spare time (!!!), he is also an amateur magician and a black belt in karate.

Graham Weihmiller, M.B.A., CFE

Graham Weihmiller joined BNI in 2014 to help execute BNI's strategic plan that includes operational enhancements, continued membership growth and ongoing global member expansion. Graham is passionate about building successful service organizations that have a remarkable value proposition and a positive social impact. Prior to BNI, he served as the CEO of a 32-year-old nationwide franchisor of homecare services. While there, he was a founding director of a foundation that provides homecare to those who cannot afford it. His previous leadership experience includes roles with Pioneer Equity Partners, American Franchise Company, Bank of America, Booz Allen and J.P. Morgan.

Graham speaks frequently on entrepreneurship and franchising and has recently been on panels at Harvard Business School, Stanford University and Georgetown University. He received his M.B.A. from Harvard Business School and his B.B.A. from the College of William & Mary. He has done subsequent executive education with Harvard Business School in India. He is a Certified Franchise Executive and active with the International Franchise Association. Graham is trained in Lean Enterprise, Process Excellence and Design for Six Sigma, and is a Six Sigma Black Belt. He is an active member of the Young Presidents Organization (YPO) and the Harvard Business School Club of Charlotte, where he was formerly the Club President. He currently serves on the BNI Foundation Board of Directors.

Robert Skrob

As a marketing expert for more than 20 years, Robert Skrob has helped thousands of businesses attract and retain their best target customers. Robert's superpower is simplification. Simplifying your message to attract more customers, simplifying what you deliver to improve long-term retention and simplifying how you deliver it to increase your profits as you scale. While he has worked with entrepreneurs in more than 100 business categories, today he specializes in helping businesses grow recurring subscription revenue. For a free guide to adding recurring subscription revenue to any business visit www.RobertSkrob.com/RecurringGrowth.

BNI

BNI, the world's largest business networking organization, was founded by Dr. Ivan Misner in 1985 as a way for businesspeople to generate referrals in a structured, professional environment. The organization, now the world's largest referral business network, has thousands of Chapters with hundreds of thousands of Members on every populated continent. Since its inception, BNI Members have passed millions of referrals, generating billions of dollars in business for the participants.

The primary purpose of the organization is to pass qualified business referrals to its Members. The philosophy of BNI may be summed up in two simple words: Givers Gain®. If you give business to people, you will get business from them. BNI allows only one person per profession to join a Chapter. The program is designed to help businesspeople develop long-term relationships, thereby creating a basis for trust and, inevitably, referrals. The mission of BNI is to help Members increase their business through a structured, positive and professional word-of-mouth program that enables them to develop long-term, meaningful relationships with quality business professionals.

To visit a Chapter near you,
contact BNI at www.bni.com.